D0708961

Books That
Change
Lives

Recommended Reading
Lists for Christian Readers

Compiled by top booksellers nationwide

Books That Change Lives: Recommended Reading Lists for Christian Readers Copyright © 2005 by Parable Press. All rights reserved. Printed in the United States of America. No part of this book may be used or reproduced in any manner whatsoever without written permission. For further information contact The Parable Group, 3563 Empleo Street, San Luis Obispo, CA 93401.

All excerpts and author quotes are used by permission.

ISBN 0-9770565-0-3

Table of Contents

Introduction

Introduction

"When I read, it's a chance to sit down with a great thinker or a great historian or an adventurer – or even an apostle – and absorb their wisdom. I don't know how many historians and philosophers I will ever have a chance to meet in this life and I certainly won't meet an apostle, but through great books, a reader has a chance to gain immeasurably from the experience and counsel of those more gifted. Good books are great roadmaps for life." ~Joni Eareckson Tada

Introducing the Personal Growth Library

Each of us can gain so much from reading the works of great Christian writers of the past. We encourage you to start your own library of classics that have changed lives and offered wisdom and inspiration to readers through the ages.

To help you begin your own library, we have carefully compiled a list of highly recommended books, chosen for depth of wisdom and their power to transform hearts and lives. Book buyers from Parable Christian Stores nationwide have given us their best recommendations. They have spent years listening to feedback from readers and watching first hand the impact of these books on lives.

Our prayer is that this guide may assist you in building a personal library to deepen your faith walk with God, and lend to others to do the same.

Chapter 1
Personal Growth Library

Thomas á Kempis (CLASSIC)
Imitation of Christ
Is it the right time in your spiritual walk to read this great classic? Written five centuries ago by a humble monk, this timeless message of faith in Christ's teachings remains a vital source of spiritual strength for people seeking to follow in the footsteps of the Lord.

Randy Alcorn
Heaven
Have you ever wondered what Heaven is really like? You may be astonished. In the most comprehensive and definitive book on Heaven to date, Randy invites you to picture Heaven the way Scripture describes it—a bright, vibrant and physical New Earth, free from sin, suffering and death and brimming with Christ's presence, wondrous natural beauty and the richness of human culture as God intended it.

Samuel Bagster
Daily Light
As Anne Graham Lotz describes it in her new introduction, this devotional is a spiritual baton to be passed down from generation to generation. It contains daily devotions, readings from the New King James Version for every morning and evening and a topical index of 60 subjects including love, hope, salvation, forgiveness and baptism.

Randy Alcorn

Randy Alcorn is a former pastor and the founder and director of Eternal Perspective Ministries (EPM), a nonprofit organization dedicated to teaching biblical truth and drawing attention to the needy and how to help them. EPM exists to meet the needs of the unreached, unfed, unborn, uneducated, unreconciled and unsupported people around the world.

"My ministry focus is communicating the strategic importance of using our earthly time, money, possessions and opportunities to invest in need-meeting ministries that count for eternity," Alcorn says. "I do that by trying to analyze, teach and apply the implications of Christian truth."

Alcorn is the author of 20 books including: *Heaven; Safely Home; Edge of Eternity; Deadline; Dominion; Pro-Life Answers to Pro-Choice Arguments; Women Under Stress* and *Money, Possessions and Eternity.*

What 5 books (other than the Bible) have had the largest impact on your life?

- *The Knowledge of the Holy* by A.W. Tozer
- *Mere Christianity* by C.S. Lewis
- *Systematic Theology* (or the condensed version, *Bible Doctrine*) by Wayne Grudem
- *The Chronicles of Narnia* by C.S. Lewis
- *Desiring God* by John Piper

Louis Berkhof (CLASSIC)
The History of Christian Doctrines
A fascinating account! Not only will you learn the origin of familiar doctrines, you will follow their journey through human history. Berkhof traces the great movements of thought within the church on such doctrines as the Trinity, the Person of Christ, sin and grace, the atonement and more.

Henry Blackaby
Experiencing God
This remarkable book has helped millions of believers renew and revitalize their love for the Lord by seeing His love for us. Awaken your awareness and understanding of His plan, His purpose and your place in His kingdom.

James M. Boice (CLASSIC)
Foundations of the Christian Faith
In one systematic volume (the revised edition of a formerly four-volume work), James Boice provides a readable overview of Christian theology for students and pastors alike, covering all the major doctrines of Christianity with scholarly rigor and a pastor's heart.

Dietrick Bonhoeffer (CLASSIC)
The Cost of Discipleship
One of the most important theologians of the twentieth century unflinchingly considers what the demands of sacrifice and ethical consistency mean to people today. "Cheap grace," Bonhoeffer wrote, "is the grace we bestow on ourselves. Costly grace is the Gospel."

Edward M. Bounds (CLASSIC)
Guide to Spiritual Warfare
Forget the image of the Devil in a red suit carrying a pitchfork. Here is a very real portrait of a very real enemy with cunning intelligence who wants to derail your faith and your life. Learn to recognize and defeat his strategies and overcome him.

Michael Card

Michael Card is an award-winning musician, performing artist and writer of *El Shaddai, Immanuel* and many other songs. He has produced over twenty albums. he has also written numerous books, including *A Violent Grace, Scribbling in the Sand, The Parable of Joy* and *Sleep Sound in Jesus* (a children's book). A graduate of western Kentucky University with a bachelor's and master's degrees in biblical studies, Card is currently at work on a Ph.D. in classical literature. He also serves as mentor to many younger artists and musicians, teaching courses on the creative process and calling the Christian recording industry into deeper discipleship. Card lives in Tennessee with his wife and four children.

What 5 books (other than the Bible) have had the largest impact on your life?

- *Cost of Discipleship* by Dietrich Bonhoeffer
- *Lion and Lamb* by Brennan Manning
- *New Testament History* by Frederick Fyvie Bruce
- *The New International Commentary on the New Testament: Mark* by William Lane
- *Count of Monte Cristo* by Alexandre Dumas

Edward M. Bounds (CLASSIC)
Power Through Prayer
The great, prayerful men of God...Wesley, Edwards, Spurgeon and others...how did they pray to receive such world-transforming results? Find out as you read their thoughts and take in helpful suggestions on getting dynamic responses from God through the power of prayer.

Jerry Bridges
Discipline of Grace
The pursuit of holiness may mean legalism and man-made rules to some; others believe that the grace of God opens the door to irresponsibility. In this sequel to *The Pursuit of Holiness*, Bridges shows how the two are anchored together.

Jerry Bridges
The Practice of Godliness
Scripture says God has given us "everything we need for life and godliness." But what makes a Christian godly? Bridges examines what it means to grow in Christian character and helps us establish the foundation upon which that character is built.

> ### Excerpt from *The Practice of Godliness*
> "Any time we stress the personal responsibility of practical actions...we are in danger of thinking that the pursuit of holiness does depend upon our own willpower, our own strength of character. Nothing is further from the truth. We are both personally responsible and totally dependent in our practice of godliness. We cannot change our hearts; that is the exclusive work of the Holy Spirit. But we can and must avail ourselves of the means he uses." [1]

Jerry Bridges
The Pursuit of Holiness
"Be holy, for I am holy," commands God to His people. Does holiness seem unattainable? You'll discover how God has equipped you to live a holy life as Bridges clarifies what we should rely on God to do and what we should accept as our own responsibility.

Philip Graham Ryken

Philip Graham Ryken is Senior Minister at Philadelphia's historic Tenth Presbyterian Church and the Bible teacher for *Every Last Word*. He received a Master of Divinity degree from Westminster Theological Seminary and has a doctorate in historical theology. Dr. Ryken is also a council member of the Alliance of Confessing Evangelicals.

He has written or edited nearly 20 books including: *Courage to Stand: Jeremiah's Battle Plan for Pagan Times*, *Is Jesus the Only Way?*, *Discovering God in Stories from the Bible*, *The Doctrines of Grace: Rediscovering the Evangelical Gospel* and *The Heart of the Cross*.

When he is not preaching or spending time with his family, he likes to read great books, shoot baskets and ponder the relationship between the Christian faith and American culture.

What 5 books (other than the Bible) have had the largest impact on your life?

- *Human Nature in Its Fourfold State* by Thomas Barton
- *Institutes of the Christian Religion* by John Calvin
- *Chronicles of Narnia* by C.S. Lewis
- *The Inspiration and Authority of Scripture* by Benjamin B. Warfield
- *The Trinity Hymnal* by Benjamin B. Warfield

Jerry Bridges
Trusting God
When hard times hit, God's sovereignty can be a comfort instead of a conundrum. This explores the scope of God's power over nations, nature and the detailed lives of individuals and helps us discern God's loving control. And as we come to know Him better, we will trust Him more completely.

Bob Briner (CLASSIC)
Roaring Lambs
Briner's manifesto states that Christians should be movers and shakers of social change—"roaring lambs"—who impact their workplace and their world with their faith. A discussion guide helps you and your friends carry out your intentions.

Brother Andrew (CLASSIC)
God's Smuggler
As a boy, Brother Andrew dreamed of being an undercover spy. As a man he found himself working undercover for God, smuggling Bibles. He prayed the border guards would not see the Bibles and they never did. Here is the amazing story of what God can do through a man of prayer.

John Bunyan (CLASSIC)
Pilgrim's Progress
The classic drama of Christian's journey to discover eternal life offers readers encouragement and direction for their own pilgrimage. Bunyan captures the speech of ordinary people as accurately as he depicts their behavior and their inner emotional and spiritual life. The tale is spiced with Bunyan's acute and satirical perceptions of the vanity and hypocrisy of his own society.

John Calvin (CLASSIC)
Institutes of the Christian Religion
Calvin's masterwork evokes strong emotions and has formed the church's understanding of Christian doctrine for generations, exerting untold influence in the development of Western thought. He fully achieves his stated desire to enable the reader to accurately handle the great doctrines and promises of the Bible.

Amy Carmichael (CLASSIC)
If

Are you ready to risk going deeper for the Lord? Dare to read this little book about Calvary love lived out in common life, based on 1 Corinthians 13. Short, hard-hitting truths about the attitude of a follower of Christ will challenge you to the core, exhorting you to comprehend and embody the love shown on the cross.

Lewis S. Chafer (CLASSIC)
Major Bible Themes

Designed for group and individual study, this provides the Biblical basis for fifty-two doctrines, with topical and Scripture indexes and discussion questions. To develop, clarify or strengthen your beliefs, this is essential for study and reference.

Oswald Chambers (CLASSIC)
My Utmost for His Highest

For nearly 75 years, millions of Christians have trusted the spiritual companionship of Oswald Chambers' classic daily devotional. These brief Scripture-based readings—by turns comforting and challenging—will draw you into God's presence. You'll treasure their insight, still fresh and vital. And you'll discover what it means to offer God your very best for His greatest purpose—to truly offer Him your utmost for His highest.

Gary Chapman
Five Love Languages

This is the breakthrough book that reveals how people express love in different ways. By teaching us how to identify and use our spouse's preferred language when we express our love for them, Dr. Chapman shows us how wonderful things can happen to relationships.

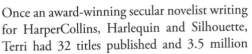

Terri Blackstock

Once an award-winning secular novelist writing for HarperCollins, Harlequin and Silhouette, Terri had 32 titles published and 3.5 million books in print. But she was miserable. Career compromises had taken their toll on her spiritual life, and she yearned to renew her relationship with Christ.

After much soul-searching, Terri told the Lord that she would never again write a work that didn't glorify Him. Since then, Terri has published more than 25 novels, including many bestsellers like the *Cape Refuge* series and *Suncoast Chronicles*. She writes about flawed Christians in crisis, primarily in the suspense genre, and she is co-author of a series of family values novels with Beverly LaHaye.

Terri has been a guest on national television programs such as *The 700 Club, At Home Live with Chuck and Jenny* and *Home Life*, as well as numerous radio programs.

What 5 books (other than the Bible) have had the largest impact on your life?

- *This Present Darkness* by Frank Peretti
- *God's Covenant* by Kay Arthur
- *Mere Christianity* by C.S. Lewis
- *My Utmost For His Highest* by Oswald Chambers
- *Lord of the Rings Trilogy* by J.R.R. Tolkien

What are you currently reading?

Bible Doctrine, by Wayne Grudem

What is your goal for writing?

"My goal in writing Christian novels is to entertain my readers with a fast-paced page-turner, while teaching truths that are woven into the plot like a fine tapestry, truths that will point my readers to Christ or challenge them to a deeper walk with Him."

Stephen Charnock (CLASSIC)
The Existence and Attributes of God
Let this seventeenth century classic bring your twenty-first century faith to a whole new level. Puritan theologian Stephen Charnock constructs an awe-inspiring portrait of God's attributes from theology and painstaking study of Scripture.

G.K. Chesterton (CLASSIC)
Orthodoxy
Chesterton described this work as a "slovenly autobiography." His humility is admirable, since this work of intellectual clarity and literary skill describes his pilgrimage to belief that orthodox Catholic Christianity was the way to satisfy his personal emotional needs and live happily in society.

Evelyn Christenson
What Happens When Women Pray
Having been tested in hundreds of prayer seminars all over the world, these teachings have enabled both men and women to learn to pray in more personal and believing ways. Move into the dynamic that occurs when people pray—it just might change your life, your family and your church.

Henry Cloud
Boundaries
Having clear boundaries is essential to a healthy, balanced lifestyle. A boundary is a personal property line that marks those things for which we are responsible. In other words, boundaries define who we are and who we are not. Discover how boundaries impact all areas of our lives: physical, mental, emotional and spiritual.

Robert Coleman
The Master Plan of Evangelism

A classic for more than 30 years, this builds on the premise that Jesus' evangelism strategies are still the best for outreach today. It shows you how following Christ's "master plan" can make you more effective at spreading the life-changing message of the Gospel.

> ### Excerpt from *The Master Plan of Evangelism*
> "Having called his men, Jesus made it a practice to be with them. This was the essence of His training program—just letting His disciples follow Him. When one stops to think of it, this was an incredibly simple way of doing it. Jesus had no formal school, no Seminaries, no outlined course of study, no periodic membership classes in which He enrolled His followers. None of these highly organized procedures considered so necessary today entered at all into His ministry. Amazing as it may seem, all Jesus did to teach these men His way was to draw them close to Himself. He was His own school and curriculum." [2]

Charles Colson
How Now Shall We Live?

Once we are transformed by a personal relationship with Jesus Christ, how do we go about transforming the world? This gives Christians the understanding, confidence and tools to confront bankrupt world views and restore and redeem every aspect of contemporary culture.

Charles Colson
Loving God

Here is a compelling, probing look at the cost of discipleship and the meaning of the first and greatest commandment. This magnificent classic will strum a deep, true chord within, even as it strips away the trappings of shallow, cultural Christianity.

L.B. Cowman (CLASSIC)
Streams in the Desert
Few books sustain such widespread recognition and perennial appeal. Mrs. Cowman's devotional is a legacy of faith and wisdom that is refreshing, relevant and trustworthy even in today's fast-paced world. Turn to it daily and let these prayerful writings lead you to the streams hidden beneath life's rocky terrain.

Jim Cymbala
Fresh Wind, Fresh Fire
Pastor Jim Cymbala shares the lessons he learned when the Spirit ignited his heart and began to move through the people at the Brooklyn Tabernacle. Transformed lives and the explosive growth of an amazing ministry will embolden you to pray for your own renewal.

Chapter 2
Personal Growth Library

Dr. James Dobson
Bringing Up Boys
Sensible advice and caring encouragement on raising boys from the nation's most trusted parenting expert, Dr. James Dobson. With so much confusion about the role of men in our society, many of us are at a loss as to how to bring up boys. Our culture has vilified masculinity and, as a result, boys are suffering. He tackles this issue with answers based on a firm foundation of Biblical principles.

Dr. James Dobson
Parenting Isn't For Cowards
This is the book frustrated parents have turned to for 15 years. Why? Because Dr. Dobson, writing as a therapist and as a parent—and drawing on a landmark study of 35,000 patients—helps parents banish guilt, protect their sanity, restore their energy and enhance their relationships with their children.

Dr. James Dobson
The New Dare to Discipline
From one generation to the next, the challenge of helping children become responsible adults doesn't change. Dobson's reassuring guide for caring parents, first released in 1970, is now updated to help a whole new generation of parents with wise counsel.

Dr. James Dobson
The New Strong-Willed Child
Dr. Dobson has revised, updated and expanded his classic bestseller for a new generation of parents and teachers. It incorporates the latest research on dealing with sibling rivalry, ADHD, low self-esteem and other important issues.

Henry Drummond (CLASSIC)
Greatest Things in the World
The one great need in our Christian life is love—more love for God and more love for each other. This book will show you how to move into the "Love Chapter" of 1 Corinthians 13 and live there.

Jonathan Edwards (CLASSIC)
Freedom of the Will
While *Sinners in the Hand of an Angry God* is his most famous work, many think *Freedom of the Will* is his best. Two-and-a-half centuries after Edwards wrote it, this book is still the most thorough argument for the complete sovereignty of God.

Jonathan Edwards (CLASSIC)
Religious Affections
Jonathan Edwards, the central figure in New England's first Great Awakening, presents a detailed description of the signs—true and false—of revival. He also dares to take a long, hard look at the evidence of true conversion and examines the controversial role emotions play in the Christian life.

Jonathan Edwards (CLASSIC)
Sinners in the Hands of an Angry God
Theologian, missionary and pastor renowned for the sermon for which the book is titled, Jonathan Edwards is considered by many historians to be the most brilliant American of his day. Explore the passionate New England preacher's penetrating spiritual insights in this attractively-bound collection of writings.

Jonathan Edwards (CLASSIC)
Works of Jonathan Edwards Volume 1 and 2
A true treasure, this is the only full edition of Edwards' works currently available. "In my early days in the ministry, there were no books which helped me more, both personally and in respect of my preaching, than this two-volume edition of *The Works of Jonathan Edwards.*" ~Dwight Moody

John Eldredge
The Journey of Desire
Can desire really be from God? "The modern church," says John Eldredge, "mistakenly teaches its people to kill desire, calling it sin and replaces it with duty or obligation." The result? Christians tend to live safe, boring lives of resignation. This groundbreaking book invites readers to rediscover God-given desire, abandon resignation and embark on an adventure he calls, "our heart's most important journey."

Excerpt from *The Journey of Desire*
"Think for a moment. The One who created you and set all those loves and gifts in your heart, the One who has shaped all your life experiences (including the ones that seem to make no sense), this God has prepared a place for you that is a more than perfect fit for all your gifts and quirks and personality traits—even those you don't know you have. Christ is not joking when he says that we shall inherit the kingdom prepared for us and shall reign with him forever. We will take the position for which we have been uniquely made and will rule as he does—meaning with creativity and power." [3]

John Eldredge
The Sacred Romance
Would you consider your relationship with God a romance? Too many believers today experience Christianity as a busyness-based religion and fail to understand that the God who saves us is also a God who woos us into a relationship of intimacy, beauty and adventure with Himself. Learn to identify the lies offered by "false loves" and journey back to the Lover of our souls.

John Eldredge
Wild at Heart
"God designed men to be dangerous," says John Eldredge. Simply look at the dreams and desires written in the heart of every boy: to be a hero, to be a warrior, to live a life of adventure and risk. Sadly, many men have buried their boyhood dreams and are often passive and bored to death. This trail-blazing book is helping men rediscover their God-given, masculine heart and is releasing them to live bold lives for the glory of God.

Elisabeth Elliott
Passion and Purity
Elisabeth Elliott teaches the often-painful yet rewarding discipline of waiting on God by candidly tracing her love story with Jim Elliott. Through letters, diary entries and memories, she shares the temptations, difficulties, victories and sacrifices of two young people whose commitment to Christ took priority.

Elisabeth Elliott
Shadow of the Almighty
This portrait of Jim Elliott, a rare and remarkable man of faith is drawn from his rich and revealing diaries, tracing the roots of his commitment to God, even knowing he might be called to an unexpected death in the prime of life. His martyrdom in 1956 shocked the nation and motivated thousands to a life of service.

Elisabeth Elliott
Through Gates of Splendor
The unforgettable true story of five men who sacrificed their lives to reach the Aucas with the Gospel. This edition includes a follow-up chapter that will give readers a unique perspective on the mysterious ways God works to perform His wonders!

Eusebius (CLASSIC)
The History of the Church from Christ to Constantine: Penguin Classics
Wouldn't it be interesting to read what happened to the church AFTER the Book of Acts? This is the only surviving account of the Church dur-

ing its crucial first 300 years from the time of Christ to the Great Persecution, written by Bishop Eusebius, a scholar and a model for all later ecclesiastical historians.

Fénelon (CLASSIC)
Talking with God
All who seek fellowship with God amid the rush and racket of modern life will find that Fénelon's searching gentleness is a wonderful pick-me-up for the heart. This selection from his letters is pure gold.

Fénelon (CLASSIC)
The Seeking Heart
Better than opening a jewel box! You will feel you have met this great man of God in person as you read this collection of his short letters to various people, imparting spiritual encouragement, counsel and sometimes reproof.

Richard Foster
Celebration of Discipline
If you're spiritually thirsty, this may be the water you're seeking. Discover the rewards of the inward disciplines of meditation, prayer, fasting and study, the outward disciplines of simplicity, solitude, submission and service and the corporate disciplines of confession, worship, guidance and celebration.

Richard Foster
Devotional Classics
Fifty-two selections introduce you to the world's great devotional writers through the course of one year. Each reading is accompanied by an introduction and meditation by Richard Foster, discussion questions and more.

John Foxe (CLASSIC)
Foxe's Book of Martyrs
With millions of copies in print, this classic of magnificent courage and faith traces the roots of religious persecution. This streamlined edition presents Foxe's work in today's language, commemorating the spiritual heroism of John Wycliffe, William Tyndale, Lady Jane Grey and many others.

Chapter 3
Personal Growth Library

Elizabeth George
A Woman After God's Own Heart
As your daily duties nudge up against each other like cars in a traffic jam, are the needs of your soul pushed aside? Elizabeth shows you how to gracefully coordinate your busy life by pursuing God's priorities first. For any woman who wants to achieve a growing relationship with God, develop an active partnership with her husband and make her home into a spiritual oasis.

Billy Graham
Angels
The world continues to be fascinated with angels...but what does the Bible say about them? With more than a million copies sold, *Angels* gives ringing assurance that we are assisted and defended by a powerful order of invisible beings.

Billy Graham
Peace With God
With quiet confidence and surefooted faith, Billy Graham points toward the One who is the only dependable source of peace that passes understanding. Both comforting and challenging, this has been changing lives for generations with chapters such as, *After Death—What?*, *Hope for the Future* and *Peace at Last*.

William Gurnall (CLASSIC)
The Christian in Complete Armour
David Wilkerson, a seasoned veteran of spiritual warfare against the forces of darkness, writes: "I believe The Christian in Complete Armour should be in the library of every man and woman of God. No Christian leader, teacher, pastor, evangelist or Christian worker should be without it." He would know! A three-volume set.

Jeanne Guyon (CLASSIC)
Experiencing the Depths of Jesus Christ
At one time this book was publicly burned in France and yet it has played a major part in the lives of more famous Christians than perhaps any other Christian book. It is still thought by many to be one of the most helpful and powerful Christian books ever written.

R. Kent Hughes
Disciplines of a Godly Man
For every man who wants to know what it means to be a Christian in today's world, this newly revised edition offers a frank Biblical discussion on family, godliness, leadership, ministry and more, using engaging illustrations, Scriptural wisdom, practical suggestions and study questions.

Charles Hummel (CLASSIC)
Tyranny of the Urgent
Like a pebble dropped in a pond, this little booklet has great impact. A classic on time management with kingdom awareness, it has turned on a light in minds worldwide as people realize the precious time lost in responding to the clamoring urgency of things that are unimportant in the light of eternity.

Hannah Hurnard (CLASSIC)
Hinds Feet on High Places
One of Hannah Hurnard's best-known and best-loved books, this allegory dramatizes the yearning of God's children to be led to new heights of love, joy and victory. Readers rejoice as Much-Afraid reaches the High Places, transformed by her union with the loving Shepherd.

> ### Excerpt from *Hinds Feet on High Places*
> "The third thing that I learned was that you, my Lord, never regarded me as I actually was, lame and weak and crooked and cowardly. You saw me as I would be when you had done what you promised and had brought me to the High Places, when it could be truly said, 'There is none that walks with such a queenly ease, nor with such grace, as she.' You always treated me with the same love and graciousness as though I were a queen already and not wretched little Much-Afraid." [4]

Bill Hybels
Becoming a Contagious Christian
Learn how to share your faith in a natural, authentic way with others who need God's love and truth. This proven action plan will show you how to impact the spiritual lives of friends, family members, co-workers and others.

Bill Hybels
Too Busy Not to Pray
We always mean to pray, but responsibilities and relationships can distract us. Pastor Bill Hybels reminds us these commitments should actually drive us to our knees. The ACTS formula (Adoration, Confession, Thanksgiving and Supplication) helps us rediscover the power and passion of prayer.

W. Phillip Keller (CLASSIC)
A Shepherd Looks at Psalm 23
Because Keller was once a shepherd, God used his experience to give him these remarkable insights into Psalm 23. Discover the expressions of love that Christ, the Great Shepherd, extends to us, "the sheep of His pasture."

Brother Lawrence (CLASSIC)
The Practice of the Presence of God
Imagine living in a home with the most breath-taking views in the world—but no windows! Such is our life if we live with our spiritual eyes closed. Brother Lawrence discovered the secret of living with a sense of God's presence and for nearly 300 years, this unparalleled classic has blessed others to do the same.

J. Gilchrist Lawson (CLASSIC)
Deeper Experiences of Famous Christians
How did famous Christians of the ages reach their mountaintop experiences of God's love and power? John Bunyan, Fénelon, Madame Guyon, D. L. Moody and many others reveal their intimate spiritual lives.

C.S. Lewis (CLASSIC)
The Abolition of Man
Lewis challenges public education by addressing a broad sweep of political, religious and philosophical concerns with razor-sharp intellect and laser-sharp wit. The modern god of relativism is forced to bow his knee to Lewis' exaltation of truth and universal values.

C.S. Lewis (CLASSIC)
The Great Divorce
Lewis exposes mankind's pathetic reasons for refusing the Lord's grace-filled invitation to enter heaven. The players in this imaginative allegory create clear portraits of human self-deception and leave an indelible memory of hell's vast loneliness and heaven's vast freedom.

C.S. Lewis (CLASSIC)
A Grief Observed
Written after his wife's tragic death as a way of surviving the "mad midnight moment," *A Grief Observed* is a beautiful and unflinchingly honest record of how even a stalwart believer can lose all sense of meaning in the universe and then gradually regain his bearings.

C.S. Lewis (CLASSIC)
Mere Christianity
Unavoidably logical and relentlessly persuasive, this intellectual introduction to Christianity uncovers common ground upon which all Christians can stand together. This forceful and accessible discussion of Christian belief has become one of the most popular introductions to Christianity and one of the most popular of Lewis' books.

Catherine Palmer

Catherine Palmer is a graduate of Southwest Baptist University and holds a master's degree in English from Baylor University. Her first book was published in 1988. Since then she has published nearly forty novels, many of them national bestsellers. Catherine has won numerous awards for her writing, including the Christy Award, the highest honor in Christian fiction. Twice she has been nominated for the Romantic Times Career Achievement Award. She has sold nearly two million copies of her novels.

With her compelling characters and strong message of Christian faith, Catherine is known for writing fiction that "touches the hearts and souls of readers." Her many collections include *A Town Called Hope, Treasures of the Heart,* the *Finders Keepers* series, and the *English Ivy* series.

What 5 books (other than the Bible) have had the largest impact on your life?

- *Heaven* by Randy Alcorn
- *Mark of the Lion* (series) by Francine Rivers
- *Christy* by Catherine Marshall
- *The Chronicles of Narnia* (series) by C.S. Lewis
- *Exodus* by Leon Uris

"Books are passports to worlds of fun, adventure, relaxation, learning and growth. Reading has literally changed my life. By reading (and memorizing parts of) the Bible, I've become a new person in Christ. My ability to understand the world, my purpose here and the history and philosophy of the ages has been strengthened by reading non-fiction. But the greatest FUN of all is fiction! Traveling to Rome in 70 AD with Francine Rivers or sipping red bush tea with Mama Precious Ramotswe in Botswana in Alexander McCall's books, or imagining the taste of (but not actually having to eat!) livermush in Jan Karon's Mitford. I can't even think what life would be like without books. Over and over, my readers write letters to me testifying how they've been changed and impacted by my books. Books have power and you can tap into that by reading! Please pick up a book and give reading a try. You'll be so glad you did!" ~Catherine Palmer, author

C.S. Lewis (CLASSIC)
Miracles

Who would have thought logic could prove miracles? C. S. Lewis uses his remarkable intellect to build a solid argument for the existence of divine intervention. This is his impeccable inquiry into the proposition that supernatural events can happen in this world.

C.S. Lewis (CLASSIC)
Space Trilogy

Lewis' acclaimed *Space Trilogy*. Includes: *Out of the Silent Planet, Perelandra and That Hideous Strength*. The remarkable Dr. Ransom is abducted by a megalomaniacal physicist and taken via spaceship to the red planet of Malacandra to be a human sacrifice. He escapes and becomes a stranger in a land enchantingly different from Earth, yet instructively similar.

C.S. Lewis (CLASSIC)
Problem of Pain

It's the universal question: Why must humanity suffer? For ourselves and for those who ask us, thank heaven for this thoughtful work by C. S. Lewis. He honestly confronts pain and suffering and provides an answer to this critical theological problem.

C.S. Lewis (CLASSIC)
The Screwtape Letters

How does the devil think? How does he tempt, blind and fool Christians? In this humorous and perceptive exchange between two devils, C. S. Lewis imparts a better understanding of how the enemy works and what it means to live a faithful life.

C.S. Lewis (CLASSIC)
Surprised By Joy
Lewis is a philosopher who thought his way to God. As an acutely perceptive observer of self, Lewis vividly recounts his spiritual journey, describing his early schooldays, his World War I experiences and his life at Oxford where he was drawn to God in a convergence of the rational and the spiritual.

C.S. Lewis (CLASSIC)
The Chronicles of Narnia
Once you enter the magical Kingdom of Narnia through the back of a humble wardrobe, you will never want to come out again until you've experienced all seven grand adventures! The Narnia stories are allegories of the great truths of the Christian faith embedded in stories that have delighted and stirred the hearts of many for generations.

C.S. Lewis (CLASSIC)
Till We Have Faces
This tale of two princesses – one beautiful and one unattractive – and the struggle between sacred and profane love is Lewis' reworking of the myth of Cupid and Psyche and one of his most enduring works.

C.S. Lewis (CLASSIC)
The Weight of Glory
Selected from sermons delivered by C. S. Lewis during World War II, these nine sermons offer guidance and inspiration in a time of great doubt, address increasing faith in any generation and provide a compassionate vision of Christianity.

Paul E. Little (CLASSIC)
Know What You Believe
A Christian's faith must be grounded in truth so they can mature in God and produce the fruit of the Spirit. This is a classic, trusted resource on the fundamental doctrines of Christianity for new believers and even longtime Christians.

Paul E. Little
Know Why You Believe
After we develop some understanding of what we believe as Christians, we can have many questions. How can I know that there is a God? Did Jesus really rise from the dead? Why is there pain and evil in the world? This book will help you find the answers.

Martin Lloyd-Jones (CLASSIC)
Studies on The Sermon on the Mount
A spiritual classic, this comprehensive study by one of the greatest expository preachers of our time explains the Sermon on the Mount and applies it to the Christian life. Vastly rich truths are gleaned for the reader's spiritual growth and great depth of thought is expressed in simple language.

Anne Graham Lotz
Just Give Me Jesus
After two pressure-filled, life-changing years of professional exhaustion and personal turmoil, Anne Graham Lotz found herself with only one heart-cry, "Please, just give me Jesus." In this faith-inspiring book, she stares intently at the realities of life with her Savior. To those needing a fresh start, to those still searching for happiness, to those in need of forgiveness, to the suffering and the self-righteous alike, Jesus was, is and will always be the answer.

Max Lucado
Grace for the Moment
For such a small book, *Grace For the Moment* has had a major impact on countless lives. With well over a million copies sold, this devotional continues to touch lives as it emphasizes the help and hope of God in everyday moments. Each daily reading features devotional writings from Max Lucado's numerous bestsellers as well as a Scripture verse selected especially for that day's reading.

Max Lucado
In the Grip of Grace
Can anything separate us from the love of God? Can you drift too far? Wait too long? Out-sin the love of God? The answer is found in one of life's sweetest words—grace. Max Lucado shows how you can't fall beyond God's love.

Max Lucado

With more than 39 million books sold worldwide, Max Lucado has touched millions with his signature storytelling writing style. Awards and accolades follow Max with each book he writes. Max is the first author to win the Gold Medallion Christian Book of the Year three times—1999 for *Just Like Jesus*, 1997 for *In the Grip of Grace* and 1995 for *When God Whispers Your Name*.

In 1994, he became the only author to have 11 of his 12 books in print simultaneously appear on paperback, hardcover and children's CBA bestseller lists. He has appeared on the Publishers Weekly, USA Today and New York Times bestseller lists.

In addition to his nonfiction books, Lucado has authored several award-winning children's titles, including, *Just In Case You Ever Wonder*, *The Crippled Lamb*, *Alabaster's Song* and the award-winning *You Are Special*. He also served as the general editor for the best-selling *Devotional Bible* and *God's Inspirational Promise Book*.

Max serves as the pulpit minister of the Oak Hills Church in San Antonio, Texas. But he says his greatest accomplishment is finding a one-in-a-million wife in Denalyn and having three unbelievable daughters: Jenna, Andrea and Sara.

What books (other than the Bible) have had the largest impact on your life?

- *The Singer* by Calvin Miller
- *Growing Strong in the Seasons of Life* by Charles R. Swindoll
- *Peculiar Treasures* by Frederick Buechner
- *Mere Christianity* by C.S. Lewis

What are you currently reading?

Leap Over a Wall by Eugene Peterson

What can you share that would encourage someone else to read more?

"Readers catch writers at their best."

Max Lucado
Just Like Jesus

God loves you just the way you are…but He refuses to leave you that way. Why? Because our ultimate goal should be a life that is just like Jesus. And with determination, faith and God's help, we can all change for the better, no matter how long the bad habits have settled in.

Max Lucado
No Wonder They Call Him Savior

Its tragedy summons all sufferers, its hope lures all searchers—no one can ignore the cross. Best-selling author Max Lucado invites readers to explore the events and circumstances surrounding our Savior on the night He was crucified.

Max Lucado
Six Hours One Friday

No matter what the storm clouds bring, you can face your pain with courage and hope. Because two thousand years ago—six hours one Friday—Christ did what was necessary to anchor you safely through all life's storms and allow you to end your voyage on the shores of eternity.

Martin Luther (CLASSIC)
The Bondage of the Will

Luther considered this to be his finest theological work. He addresses what he saw as the heart of the Gospel: Our inability to save ourselves; the sovereignty of divine grace in salvation; justification by faith; and predestination as determined by the foreknowledge of God.

Martin Luther (CLASSIC)

Luther's Small Catechism

Considered "the layman's Bible," Luther's Small and Large Catechisms contain "everything which …a Christian must know for his salvation." Rich with Luther's vivid language, this contemporary New International Version translation includes an appendix, a description of Lutheran confessional writings and a topical index.

Erwin Lutzer

Erwin W. Lutzer is senior pastor of The Moody Church in Chicago. A graduate of Dallas Theological Seminary and Loyola University, he is the author of numerous books, including the Gold Medallion award winner *Hitler's Cross* and the bestseller *One Minute After You Die*. He is also a teacher on radio programs heard on more than 700 stations throughout the United States and the world, including Songs in the Night, The Moody Church Hour, and the daily feature Running to Win. He and his wife, Rebecca, live in the Chicago area and have three married children and six grandchildren.

What 5 books (other than the Bible) have had the largest impact on your life?

- *The Bondage of the Will* by Martin Luther
- *The Adversary* by Mark Bubeck
- *The Pleasures of God* by John Piper
- *Desiring God* by John Piper
- *Whatever Happened to the Human Race* by Francis Schaeffer

Chapter 4
Personal Growth Library

Brennen Manning
Ragamuffin Gospel
Many believers agonize over failures and pull away from God because they believe He is disappointed in them. In this repackaged edition—now with full appendix, study questions and the author's epilogue—Brenning shows that nothing could be further from the truth.

Brennen Manning
Ruthless Trust
How do we overcome our fears and doubts? "Learn to trust God," says the author, "and be more fully open to the promise of divine love. If we unite our faith and hope, the yield is greater trust in God." Written in the refreshingly honest tone that made *The Ragamuffin Gospel* so successful and readable, Manning leads his readers to the next level, calling on them to shed the limitations of fear, shame and doubt and put their trust in God's unconditional love.

Peter Marshall
Light and the Glory
Did God have a plan for America? The *Light and the Glory* answers this question and many more as it looks at our nation's history from God's point of view, giving us new inspiration to fulfill God's intentions for our country. Discover the United States' true national heritage!

Walter Martin (CLASSIC)
The Kingdom of the Cults
Since 1965, this is the leading reference work on the major contemporary cult systems. With substantial new information evaluating each cult's history and contrasting their teaching with true Biblical theology, it is essential in dealing with cults at home and overseas.

David McCasland (CLASSIC)
Oswald Chambers: Abandoned to God
Like a celestial bell rung from on high, the life of Oswald Chambers resounds sweetly through history, urging everyone to do 'their utmost for God's highest.' As author of more than thirty books, all but one compiled by his wife, Chambers preached and taught with stunning spiritual impact.

Josh McDowell
A Ready Defense
Be prepared to stand firm against challenges to the truth. Josh McDowell offers sword-sharp defenses in 60 of the most-challenged areas of faith in one, easy-to-reference volume. This is excellent for all believers and extremely helpful for college students.

Josh McDowell
More than a Carpenter
Josh McDowell used to argue persuasively and passionately against Jesus. Now he argues persuasively and passionately for Him and can help you to do the same. This hard-hitting book will help you talk with people who are skeptical about Jesus' deity, His resurrection and His claims on their lives.

Robert McGee
The Search for Significance
In this re-launch of the timeless, two million-selling classic, you will gain new skills for getting off the performance treadmill, discover how four false beliefs have negatively impacted your life and learn how to overcome obstacles that prevent you from experiencing the truth of self-worth.

Andrew Murray (CLASSIC)
Abide in Christ

Murray believed many Christians hesitate at the door of God's throne room instead of accepting God's invitation to come in. He knew what it meant to be continually in the Father's presence and in these 31 heart-searching readings based on John 15, he shares how to live in fellowship with Jesus.

Andrew Murray (CLASSIC)
Absolute Surrender

Do you yearn to delight in the fellowship of Jesus and discover victory over sin? First published more than a century ago, this book has allowed thousands to discover that victory and unbroken fellowship with Jesus are only a step away.

Andrew Murray (CLASSIC)
God's Best Secrets

In this devotional, Murray shares the personal revelation he gained from spending quiet time alone with God. Discover the secrets of fellowship, prayer, faith and more as you enter into the wonderful privileges revealed in *God's Best Secrets*.

Andrew Murray (CLASSIC)
Humility

This frank discussion of humility was written by a man qualified to write it. He admits his pride was so great that he tried to stop a revival for which his father had prayed for sixty years! God ultimately taught him humility and its relation to faith, holiness and happiness and he shares it all in this book.

Andrew Murray (CLASSIC)
With Christ in the School of Prayer

Prepare yourself for intercessory prayer. Using Jesus' teaching on prayer as a model, Murray expounds on the secret of believing in prayer, the certainty of answered prayer, the power of prevailing prayer and the chief end of prayer. This special revised edition includes a timeline of history and an illustrated biography.

Bruce Wilkinson

Bruce Wilkinson serves as the chairman of Dream for Africa, Global Vision Resources and Ovation Productions. With over 22 million combined copies sold and two No. 1 New York Times bestsellers, Bruce Wilkinson has a track record of record-setting books. He is the author of *The Prayer of Jabez*, *Secrets of the Vine* and *The Dream Giver*, as well as many other books.

He has spoken around the world and been featured as a guest on numerous television shows. He founded Walk Thru the Bible Ministries, a global, trans-denominational Christian organization. Bruce and his wife, Darlene Marie, have three children and six grandchildren. They divide their time between Georgia and South Africa.

What 5 books (other than the Bible) have had the largest impact on your life?
- *Hudson Taylor and the China Inland Mission* (2 volume set) by Dr. & Mrs. Howard Taylor
- *My Utmost for His Highest* by Oswald Chambers
- *Charles Haddon Spurgeon's Autobiography* (4 volume set)
- *Absolute Surrender* by Andrew Murray
- *The Knowledge of the Holy* by A.W. Tozer

Iain H. Murray (CLASSIC)
David Martyn Lloyd-Jones:
The First Forty Years 1899-1939
The events that moved Martyn Lloyd-Jones from a glamorous Harley Street medical practice to a pastorate in an impoverished Welsh mining town make intriguing and inspiring reading.

Iain H. Murray (CLASSIC)
David Martyn Lloyd-Jones:
The Fight of Faith 1939-1981
This volume begins as the ministry of Martyn Lloyd-Jones at Westminster Chapel suddenly changes. His hard work during the war years becomes foundational to his great influence in London and eventually in even wider circles...universities, Europe, America, South Africa and in his books, to the whole world.

Iain H. Murray (CLASSIC)
Jonathan Edwards: A New Biography
Edwards' theology is shown in the natural context of his everyday life as we follow him both in public and in private through his days as a pastor in the Great Awakening and through his "wilderness" years in the Stockbridge outpost.

Watchman Nee (CLASSIC)
The Normal Christian Life
Watchman Nee simplifies Ephesians into memorable and practical statements based on three key ideas: Our position in Christ is one of sitting, our life in the world is one of walking and our attitude toward Satan is one of standing. "We do not fight for victory, we fight from victory."

Henri Nouwen (CLASSIC)
The Return of the Prodigal Son: A Story of Homecoming
The lessons are many in this powerful drama of fatherhood, filial duty, rivalry and anger between brothers and they are all eloquently taught by this beloved spiritual writer. As he meditates in writing on this parable, he fluently imparts its enduring lessons for believers.

Stormie Omartian
The Power of a Praying Wife

Today's challenges and pressures can make a fulfilling marriage seem like an impossible dream. Yet God delights in doing the impossible if only we would ask. Stormie Omartian shares how God has strengthened her own marriage since she began to pray for her husband concerning key areas of his life.

Excerpt from *The Power of a Praying Wife*

"When we live by the power of God rather than our flesh, we don't have to strive for power with our words. "For the kingdom of God is not in word but in power" (1 Corinthians 4:20). It's not the words we speak that make a difference, it is the power of God accompanying them. You'll be amazed at how much power your words have when you pray before you speak them. You'll be even more amazed at what can happen when you shut up and let God work." [5]

Fulton Oursler (CLASSIC)
The Greatest Story Ever Told

In this highly regarded 1949 account about the life of Jesus, Oursler imbued the Gospels with life, embellished them with descriptive detail, dialogue and personality and captured the essence of the compassionate yet forceful Son of God and His mission.

Chapter 5
Personal Growth Library

J.I. Packer
Faithfulness and Holiness: The Witness of J.C. Ryle
As heir to a fortune, J. C. Ryle had a hopeful future until the day his father declared bankruptcy. Along with a reprint of Ryle's classic, Holiness, are J.I. Packer's own reflections on the life of one of the most influential evangelical leaders of the 19th century.

J.I. Packer
Knowing God
The Apostle Paul counted everything in his life as rubbish in comparison with knowing Jesus Christ. In this updated and revised edition of Packer's classic, you will discover the difference between knowing God and knowing about Him.

J.B. Phillips (CLASSIC)
Your God is Too Small
In a world expanded to the point of bewilderment by global events and scientific discoveries, our idea of God must expand beyond "Resident Policeman," "Grand Old Man," "Managing Director" or any of the other small, inadequate boxes we try to fit Him into.

> **Excerpt from *Knowing God***
> "It is a staggering thing, but it is true—the relationship in which sinful human beings know God is one in which God, so to speak, takes them on to his staff, to be henceforth His fellow-workers (see 1 Cor 3:9) and personal friends. The action of God in taking Joseph from prison to become Pharaoh's prime minister is a picture of what he does to every Christian: from being Satan's prisoner, he finds himself transferred to a position of trust in the service of God. At once life is transformed. Whether being a servant is matter for shame or for pride depends on whose servant one is." [6]

Arthur W. Pink (CLASSIC)
Attributes of God

"Tell me a little about yourself!" Friendships and job interviews begin with this interested invitation. In these pages, Pink tells us wondrous things about the Lord—His characteristics and attributes—so we can meet our greatest personal and salvational need—to truly, thoroughly know and love God.

Arthur W. Pink (CLASSIC)
Sovereignty of God

In many modern books, especially those that address the issue of pain and calamity, the subject of God's ultimate control is addressed. This is a classic on the subject of sovereignty, honoring God with His proper place of supremacy.

John Piper
A Godward Life

One hundred and twenty vignettes focus on the radical consequences of living with God at the center of all we do. Steeped in Scripture, this is a passionate and articulate call for believers to live in conscious and glad submission to the sovereignty and glory of God.

John Piper

ECPA Gold Medallion winner John Piper is the Pastor for Preaching at Bethlehem Baptist Church in Minneapolis, Minnesota. He grew up in Greenville, South Carolina, and studied at Wheaton College, where he first sensed God's call to enter the ministry. He went on to earn degrees from Fuller Theological Seminary (B.D.) and the University of Munich (D.theol.). For six years he taught Biblical Studies at Bethel College in St. Paul, Minnesota, and in 1980 accepted the call to serve as pastor at Bethlehem.

John is the author of more than 20 books including *When I Don't Desire God, Desiring God, Don't Waste Your Life, A Hunger for God* and *The Passion of Jesus Christ*. His preaching and teaching is featured on the daily radio program *Desiring God*. He and wife Noël have four sons, one daughter and four grandchildren.

**What books (other than the Bible)
have had the largest impact on your life?**

- *Hermeneutics* by Daniel Fuller
- *The Unity of the Bible* by Daniel Fuller
- *Validity in Interpretation* by E.D. Hirsch
- *How to Read a Book* by Mortimer Adler and Charles Van Doren
- *Mere Christianity* by C.S. Lewis
- *Screwtape Letters* by C.S. Lewis
- *The Lion,The Witch and The Wardrobe* by C.S. Lewis
- *Freedom of Will* by Jonathan Edwards
- *Dissertation Concerning the End for Which God Created the World* by Jonathan Edwards
- *The Presence of the Future* by George Ladd

John Piper
Desiring God

In this paradigm-shattering classic, newly revised and expanded, John Piper reveals that the debate between duty and delight doesn't truly exist: Delight is our duty. Readers will embark on a dramatically different and joyful experience of their faith.

John Piper
Don't Waste Your Life

It's easy to slip through life without taking any risks—without making your life count. But life is short and precious; it shouldn't be wasted. You don't need to know a lot to make a lasting difference in the world, but you do have to know the few great, unchanging and glorious things that matter—and be willing to live and die for them.

Leonard Ravenhill (CLASSIC)
Why Revival Tarries

Appalled by the disparity between the New Testament church and the church today, Leonard Ravenhill, one of the twentieth century's greatest authorities on revival, sounded a no-compromise call to believers. His message is drastic, fearless, often radical and as timely as when it was published nearly fifty years ago.

Alan Redpath (CLASSIC)
Victorious Christian Life

Chapter by chapter, Redpath uses the book of Joshua to demonstrate how to enter God's promised land and enjoy victorious Christian living, noting that the whole land of Canaan was given to the people of Israel, but they possessed only the portion they claimed.

Don Richardson
Peace Child

How do you communicate the Gospel to cannibalistic people who not only condone cruelty and treachery, but honor them as ideals? Determined to find a way, the Richardsons approached the Sawi tribe in 1962, armed only with the story of God's "Peace Child." A gripping account of God's faithfulness.

J. Otis Ledbetter

J. Otis Ledbetter is the senior pastor of Sonrise Church in Clovis, California, a congregation he has served for the last eighteen years. In addition to his church ministry, he is a co-founder and chairman of the board of Heritage Builders Association, a ministry of Focus on the Family. The goal of this eight-year-old ministry is to continue to develop and maintain a cooperative network of families and churches committed to passing a solid Christian heritage to the next generation. As part of his work with Heritage Builders, Ledbetter specializes in leading workshops, which teach parents and grandparents the spiritual, emotional and social aspects of the legacy they will leave.

Ledbetter, who holds a PhD in education from Louisiana Baptist University, has been featured on The 700 Club, Thomas Road Baptist's TV Angel Network show, the Moody Broadcasting Network and several other radio and television outlets. In addition to authoring several books, he has written numerous magazine articles and is a frequent conference speaker.

What 5 books (other than the Bible) have had the largest impact on your life?
- *A Spiritual Clinic* by J. Oswald Sanders
- *Breaking Free from the Bondage of Sin* by Henry Brandt
- *Eternity in Their Hearts* by Don Richardson
- *Mere Christianity* by C.S. Lewis
- *What is God Like?* by Eugenia Price

Fritz Ridenour (CLASSIC)
So What's the Difference?
Did you ever wonder what the difference is? Revised and updated to help Christians better understand their own beliefs, this 1967 explanatory classic offers straightforward, non-critical comparisons of the basic tenets of the major world religions.

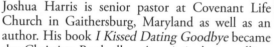
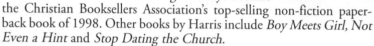
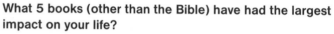

Joshua Harris is senior pastor at Covenant Life Church in Gaithersburg, Maryland as well as an author. His book *I Kissed Dating Goodbye* became the Christian Booksellers Association's top-selling non-fiction paperback book of 1998. Other books by Harris include *Boy Meets Girl, Not Even a Hint* and *Stop Dating the Church.*

What 5 books (other than the Bible) have had the largest impact on your life?
- *Holiness* by J.C. Ryle
- *Knowing God* by J.I. Packer
- *The Cross & Christianity* by D.A. Carson
- *A Call to Spiritual Reform* by D.A. Carson
- *Bible Doctrine* by Wayne Grudem

Frances Roberts (CLASSIC)
Come Away My Beloved
Be swept away by His love. *Come Away My Beloved* ministers encouragement, hope, comfort and conviction to both new Christians and long-time believers seeking spiritual renewal, leading you deeper into devotion to the Lord.

J.C.Ryle (CLASSIC)
Holiness
With his trademark candor, J.C. Ryle strips away the pious ornamentation that many confuse for holiness and unfolds the true beauty of being made holy by God. The first unabridged edition in decades, it includes a foreword by D. Martyn Lloyd-Jones and an exhaustive index of Scripture.

Charles Ryrie (CLASSIC)
Basic Theology
Wouldn't it be wonderful to understand theology without all the jargon associated with it? Dr. Ryrie strips down the heavy terms to the simple language of explanation and arrives at certainty. This is, after all, the purpose of Scriptural doctrine: "…so that you may know that you have eternal life." 1 John 5:13

Chapter 6
Personal Growth Library

J. Oswald Sanders
Spiritual Leadership
Be motivated to press on in service for Jesus Christ and place your talents and powers at God's disposal, so you can become a leader used for His glory. In modern language, this classic illustrates Biblical leadership principles and helps to apply them.

Francis Schaeffer (CLASSIC)
25 Basic Bible Studies
Study the Bible with one of the most influential Christian thinkers of our century. Dr. Schaeffer groups Scripture into themes to show how God's Word addresses real people with real problems and offers real solutions. Expanded to include Schaeffer's classic, *No Final Conflict.*

Francis Schaeffer (CLASSIC)
Escape From Reason
Many today are without God and sinking into despair, escaping into a fantasy world of experience, drugs and pornography. In this highly original book, Dr. Schaeffer traces the roots of the humanistic reasoning now blossoming in our literature, art and music, theatre and cinema, television and popular culture.

Francis Schaeffer (CLASSIC)
He is There and Is Not Silent
It is a divine paradox that the ceaseless noise of the world masks the silent despair of modern life, while the hush of the heavens resounds with truth to those who will listen. Here are answers for fundamental questions about God, such as who He is and why He matters.

Francis Schaeffer (CLASSIC)
How Should We Then Live?
As one of the foremost evangelical thinkers of the twentieth century, Francis Schaeffer long pondered the fate of declining Western culture, analyzed the reasons for modern society's state of affairs and presented the only viable alternative: Living by the Christian ethic and accepting the Bible's morals, values and meaning.

Francis Schaeffer (CLASSIC)
Mark of a Christian
Bumper stickers are great, but Christians are supposed to be known by their love. Schaeffer confronts the not-so-pretty picture of Christianity sometimes presented to the world and challenges, "The world has turned away. Is there then no way to make the world look again—this time at true Christianity?"

Francis Schaeffer (CLASSIC)
The God Who is There
Where did the clashing ideas about God, science, history and art come from and where are they going? For over thirty years, this landmark book has changed the way the church sees the world, demonstrating how Christianity can confront the competing philosophies around the globe.

Ryan Dobson

Ryan Dobson's hands-on knowledge of youth culture and speaking experience has propelled him to the forefront of today's younger generation. Ryan travels extensively, speaking more than one hundred times a year at events ranging from music festivals, concert tours, youth camps and crisis pregnancy center fundraisers. His outspokenness has landed him hundreds of radio and TV interviews.

Ryan's first book, *Be Intolerant*, examined moral relativism and its role in society today. It quickly became a top 20 ECPA bestseller. His most recent release, *To Die For*, invites readers to leave their empty lives behind to live an adventure-filled life following Christ.

The son of James and Shirley Dobson, Ryan graduated from Biola University with a bachelor's degree in communications. He lives in Southern California, where he loves to surf and skateboard with friends.

What 5 books (other than the Bible) have had the largest impact on your life?

- *How Should We Then Live?* by Francis Schaeffer
- *Waking the Dead* by John Eldredge
  (read EVERYTHING John has written)
- *Making Sense Out of Suffering* by Peter Kreeft
  (*Three Philosophies of Life* is great, too)
- *Dating Secrets of the Ten Commandments* by
  Rabbi Shmuley Boteach
- *Love Must Be Tough* by Dr. James Dobson (Come on, you think I'd leave my own Dad out of this? Seriously though, this is a must have for anyone in a relationship of any kind)

"There are so many great books to choose from, but I chose Francis Schaeffer for its timelessness. This was on the required reading list from Summit Ministries. It was great when I first read it and it's almost prophetic now. The first book I read by John Eldredge was *Sacred Romance*. I loved it, but *Wild at Heart* changed my life. I'd have put this on my list if it wasn't for *Waking the Dead*. But, you all should really read both, then move on to the rest of his books. Peter Kreeft is an amazing philosopher and author. More people should know and read him. I was just given the book by Rabbi Boteach and it is HILARIOUS!! It also makes great points, too. Lastly, but certainly not least, is my dad's book. Most people who read this are married, but that should change. The chapter on dating is AWESOME. Read it! I hope you enjoy these books."

Francis Schaeffer (CLASSIC)
True Spirituality

A treasure trove of wisdom for Christians trying to discover what true spirituality looks like in everyday life! Celebrate the thirtieth anniversary of this twentieth-century spiritual classic with a special commemorative edition featuring a new foreword by Chuck Colson.

Dutch Sheets
Intercessory Prayer

Have you ever wondered if your prayers really count? Or why you never seem to get any answers? If so, *Intercessory Prayer* will provide hope and convince you that your prayers can indeed move heaven and earth.

Charles Sheldon (CLASSIC)
In His Steps

The classic is the work of Christian fiction that coined the phrase, "What would Jesus do?" For the first time in their lives, Rev. Henry Maxwell and his congregation are forced to consider this question and its consequences. No one in town is left untouched by the results.

Bruce Shelley (CLASSIC)
Church History in Plain Language

It's about time someone wrote a church history about people, not just "eras" and "ages." This taps the roots of the Christian family tree, combining authoritative research with a captivating style.

Hannah Whithall Smith (CLASSIC)
A Christian's Secret to a Happy Life
Loved for nearly a century and a half, this book has helped millions of believers realize their Creator has given them the strength and spirit to move beyond life's difficulties and attain the shining happiness that is Christianity's promise.

Excerpt from *A Christian's Secret to a Happy Life*
"An old writer says, 'All discouragement is from the devil;' and I wish every Christian would take this as a motto and would realize that he must fly from discouragement as he would from sin. But if we fail to recognize the truth about temptation, this is impossible; for if the temptations are our own fault, we cannot help being discouraged. But they are not. The Bible says, 'Blessed is the man that endureth temptation'; and we are exhorted to 'count it all joy when we fall in to diverse temptations.' Temptation, therefore, cannot be sin; and the truth is, it is no more a sin to hear these whispers and suggestions of evil in our souls than it is for us to hear the wicked talk of bad men as we pass them on the street. The sin comes, in either case, only by our stopping and joining in with them." [7]

R.C. Sproul
Chosen by God
Here is a clear Scriptural case for the classic and often controversial Christian doctrine of predestination. Through this view of a truly sovereign God, readers will see how sinfulness prevents man from choosing God on his own; instead, God must change people's hearts.

R.C. Sproul
Essential Truths of the Christian Faith
With the layperson in mind, Dr. Sproul offers a basic understanding of the Christian faith and brief explanations of Biblical concepts every Christian should know, in language everyone can understand. Highlighted with homespun analogies and 100+ doctrines categorized under easy-reference headings.

R.C. Sproul
The Holiness of God
Just when we relax into the embrace of grace, we tense up when we consider the awesome holiness of God. Sproul's classic, now expanded and updated, eases the tension between God's terrifying holiness and His comforting mercy.

R.C. Sproul
What's in the Bible
Theologian R.C. Sproul and best-selling author Robert Wolgemuth collaborate to present an overview of the entire Bible. The resulting roadmap highlights the essence of God's voice, activity and purpose throughout the Old and New Testaments in a thoroughly readable form.

Charles Haddon Spurgeon (CLASSIC)
Holy Spirit Power
The miraculous new life of the early Christians amazed the world and turned it upside down. You can experience the same kind of newness and power in your walk with God as you learn how the Holy Spirit can be your ever-present Friend and mighty Helper.

Charles Haddon Spurgeon (CLASSIC)
Morning and Evening
For tens of thousands of Christians over the last century, this has served as their daily devotional guide through life's ups and downs.

Excerpt from *Morning and Evening*
"Are you mourning, believer, because you are so weak in the divine life: because your faith is so small and your love so feeble? Cheer up, for you have cause for gratitude. Remember that in some things you are equal to the greatest and most full-grown Christian. You are as much bought with blood as he is. You are as much an adopted child of God as any other believer. An infant is as truly a child of its parents as is the full-grown man. You are as completely justified, for your justification is not a thing of degrees: your little faith has made you every bit as clean." [8]

Charles Haddon Spurgeon (CLASSIC)
Spurgeon on Prayer & Spiritual Warfare
Answered prayers and a deeper faith in God await you as you implement these vital truths. Charles Spurgeon gives us the keys to prayer, praising God and warring against Satan so we can live a successful Christian life.

Charles Haddon Spurgeon (CLASSIC)
Treasury of David
Plunge into Spurgeon's great commentary on the Book of Psalms and drink deeply of the Living Water. Every word of Spurgeon's own *Exposition* is updated. *Hints to Preachers* is displayed in outline form for preachers, crossed-referenced to Spurgeon's numbered sermons to aid further study.

St. Augustine (CLASSIC)
City of God
One of the great cornerstones in the history of Christian philosophy, *City of God* provides an insightful interpretation of the development of modern Western society and thought. Contrasting earthly and heavenly cities, Augustine explores human history in its relation to all eternity.

St. Augustine (CLASSIC)
Confessions
Augustine's autobiography is a moving and profound record of a human soul. The most widely read of all his works, it reveals both his struggles with faith and his love for his Master. He speaks to the heart of humanity about our weakness and frailty, our depravity and our need for a holy God.

George Steer (CLASSIC)
George Mueller: Delighted in God
Never once advertising or making known his financial needs—except in prayer to God—George Mueller housed and fed thousands of homeless children in England. Here is the life story of the man who lived by prayer and faith alone.

John R. Stott
Basic Christianity
Here's the nutshell we're always talking about things being in. In this classic little book, Stott presents the fundamentals of Christianity and urges the non-Christian to consider the claims of Christ.

John R. Stott
The Cross of Christ
"I could never myself believe in God, if it were not for the cross...In the real world of pain, how could one worship a God who was immune to it?" With compelling honesty, John Stott confronts this generation with the centrality of the cross in God's redemption of the world.

Alexander Strauch
Biblical Eldership
Elders play a critical role in our churches, supporting the pastor and serving the congregation. This practical book explains the categories of eldership, the duties and qualifications and even their relationships with each other. Excellent for choosing the right people to serve in this capacity.

Lee Strobel
Case for a Creator
Has science discovered God? At the very least, it's giving faith an immense boost as new findings emerge about the incredible complexity of our universe. Lee Strobel reexamines the theories that once led him away from God. Through his compelling account, you'll encounter the mind-stretching discoveries from cosmology to DNA research that present astonishing evidence in *The Case for a Creator*.

Lee Strobel
Case for Christ
Using the dramatic scenario of an investigative journalist pursuing his story and leads, Strobel uses his experience as an award-winning reporter for the Chicago Tribune to interview experts about the evidence for Christ from the fields of science, philosophy and history.

Alison Strobel

Alison Strobel is a novelist and former elementary educator. Her father, best-selling and award-winning author Lee Strobel, instilled her with a love of stories at a young age. Alison and her husband live in California.

What 5 books (other than the Bible) have had the largest impact on your life?

- *Microserfs* by Douglas Coupland
- *A Voice in the Wind* by Francine Rivers
- *Walking on Water* by Madeline L'Engle
- *A Tree Grows in Brooklyn* by Betty Smith
- *To Kill A Mockingbird* by Harper Lee

What can you share that would encourage someone else to read more?

"The ability to read is such a gift. No other medium allows us to so completely "disappear" into a different life. Movies do all the work for you; your imagination has nothing to do, because all the images are already there and you're just watching blankly. Music, which is my second love next to books (both reading and writing them) comes close, but songs are so short! Just when you're really into it, it's over. But books...books open entire worlds to you. They allow you to be people you'll never get to be, meet people you'll never get to meet, go places you'll never get to go...what an opportunity! And it's not just an opportunity to escape your own life; it's an opportunity to learn, to walk in someone else's shoes and see what life is like for others."

Lee Strobel
Case for Faith
This eagerly anticipated sequel to Lee Strobel's best-selling *The Case for Christ* finds the author investigating the nettlesome issues and doubts of the heart that threaten faith. Eight major topics are addressed including doubt, the problem of pain and the existence of evil.

Richard Swenson
Margin
Dr. Richard Swenson sees a steady stream of exhausted, hurting people coming into his office suffering from the societal epidemic of "living without margin." Here, he offers an overall strategy for health that involves contentment, simplicity, balance and rest.

Charles R. Swindoll
Intimacy with the Almighty
From his own personal journal, Charles Swindoll offers all-new insights to guide readers on a journey to intimacy with God. This keepsake book with an embossed, antique-looking cover includes pages in Swindoll's handwriting.

Joni Eareckson Tada
Joni - An Unforgettable Story
In this award-winning classic of faith's triumph over adversity, Joni reveals the meaning of her life and the special ways God reveals His love. This 25th Anniversary Edition describes her life since the book's publication in 1976, including her marriage to Ken Tada and the expansion of her worldwide ministry.

Howard Taylor (CLASSIC)
Hudson Taylor's Spiritual Secrets
This account of missionary Hudson Taylor's amazing life has been an inspiration to many. This little book is huge in terms of its presentation of a life lived exclusively by faith in God to supply every need of a missionary outreach to inland China.

Joni Eareckson Tada

Joni Eareckson Tada is the founder of Joni and Friends, an organization accelerating Christian ministry in the disability community. A diving accident in 1967 left her a quadriplegic in a wheelchair and during two years of rehabilitation, she learned how to paint with a brush between her teeth. Her high detail fine art paintings and prints are sought after and collected.

She is a popular conference speaker both in the US and overseas and the author of over 30 books. Her best-selling and award-winning works cover topics ranging from disability outreach to reaching out to God and include: *A Christmas Longing, Life and Death Dilemma, Heaven ...Your Real Home, The God I Love* and her biography, *Joni*.

She has also written several children's books, including *Tell Me The Promises*, which received the Evangelical Publishers' Association's Gold Medallion and Silver Medal in the 1997 C.S. Lewis Awards, and *Tell Me The Truth* which received the EP Gold Medallion.

What 5 books (other than the Bible) have had the largest impact on your life?

- *The Reformed Doctrine of Predestination* by Loraine Boettner
- *Holiness* by Bishop J. C. Ryle
- *Grace Grows Best in Winter* by Margaret Clarkson
- *The Book of Common Prayer*
- *Knowing God* by J. I. Packer

Corrie Ten Boom (CLASSIC)
The Hiding Place

Corrie Ten Boom's wondrous story tells of God's ability to illuminate the dark recesses of despair and foster forgiveness in a wounded heart. Corrie's saga of surviving the Ravensbruck concentration camp and moving into a life of miraculous ministry is a story for all Christians for all time.

W. Ian Thomas
Saving Life of Christ

Wherever you are in your spiritual growth, you can always go farther. This book, with deep reverence for its subject, takes readers on a journey to discover the deeper meanings of the Christian life.

A.W. Tozer (CLASSIC)
Attributes of God

Inspirational reading at its best. The chapters of this book were originally sermons preached by Tozer. Whether spoken or written, his words "promote personal heart religion" among God's people. You will learn about 10 attributes of God, including goodness, mercy and grace.

A.W. Tozer (CLASSIC)
The Knowledge of the Holy

If the title intimidates you, you're not alone; however, these pages contain wonderful knowledge of the nature of God and how we can recapture a sense of His awesome majesty. Rejuvenate your prayer life, meditate more reverently, understand God more deeply and experience His presence in your daily life.

A.W. Tozer (CLASSIC)
The Pursuit of God

In his own time, Tozer was called the "twentieth-century prophet." Winner of the ECPA Platinum Book Award, this book is perhaps his greatest legacy to the church. Let its seeds of wisdom take root in your spirit and bear fruit for God.

Patricia Hickman

Patricia Hickman is an award-winning novelist, a part-time speaker, a pastor's wife and a mother. Her books include the popular *Land of the Far Horizons* series, *Fallen Angels*, *The Touch* and *Katrina's Wings*. Patricia's novels have received critical acclaim and earned her multiple awards, including two Silver Angel Awards for Excellence in Media.

What 5 books (other than the Bible) have had the largest impact on your life?

- *Reaching For the Invisible God* by Philip Yancey
- *The Hiding Place* by Corrie Ten Boom
- *Mere Christianity* by C.S. Lewis
- *A Grace Disguised* by Gerry Sittser
- *Tuesdays With Morrie* by Mitch Albom

What can you share that would encourage someone else to read more?

"I like to encourage reading, not just for the sake of escapism, although I search for that kind of enjoyment in reading, but to see the world through the perspective of another life unlike my own. I would encourage readers, of course, to read, but read about places, people and circumstances that are different from your corner of the world. Don't be afraid to read about pain and suffering along with joy and romance. You can't have one without the other. Read from the heart of the writer who has to share from a less-than-pristine life. That is the springboard for redemption—God reaching into the darkest places and lifting us out of doom. That is true joy and true romance, from the Savior to the Bride and from the writer to the reader."

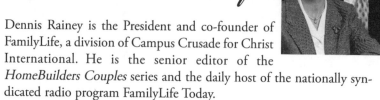

Dennis Rainey

Dennis Rainey is the President and co-founder of FamilyLife, a division of Campus Crusade for Christ International. He is the senior editor of the *HomeBuilders Couples* series and the daily host of the nationally syndicated radio program FamilyLife Today.

He is the co-author, with wife Barbara, of several books including: *Moments Together for Couples, The New Building Your Mate's Self-Esteem, Parenting Today's Adolescent, Two Hearts are Better Than One, Starting Your Marriage Right, Growing a Spiritually Strong Family, Two Hearts Praying as One* and the new *Pressure Proof Your Marriage.*

What books (other than the Bible) have had the largest impact on your life?
- *Humility: The Beauty of Holiness* by Andrew Murray
- *7 Habits of Highly Successful People* by Stephen Covey
- *Chronicles of Narnia* by C.S. Lewis
- *The Princess & The Goblin* by George MacDonald
- *The Knowledge of the Holy* by A.W. Tozer
- *The Seven Laws of Teaching* by John Milton Gregory
- *Spiritual Leadership* by Oswald Chambers
- *Experiencing God Workbook* by Henry Blackaby
- *The Pursuit of God* by A.W. Tozer
- *Quiet Talks on Prayer* by S.D. Gordon

Henry Blackaby

Henry Blackaby, president of Blackaby Ministries International, has provided leadership to thousands. Devoting his lifetime to ministry, he has served as a music director, education director and pastor. He led revival and spiritual awakening at the North American Mission Board of the Southern Baptist Convention. Now officially retired, Dr. Blackaby continues to provide consultative leadership. He has published many spiritually influential messages, most notably *Experiencing God*, which has sold more than four million copies and has been translated into over 45 languages. He and his wife have five children, all serving in the ministry. His long-range goal is to encourage revival and spiritual awakening around the world.

Dr. Blackaby's Recommended Reading List

Faith
Blackaby, Henry - *What The Spirit Is Saying to the Churches*
Huegel, F.J. - *Forever Triumphant*
Muller, George - *The Autobiography of George Muller*
Sauer, Erich - *In the Arena of Faith*
Stewart, James - *A Faith to Proclaim*

Family
Blackaby, Henry & Blackaby, Marilynn - *Experiencing God as Couples*
Murray, Andrew - *Raising Your Child to Love God*
Spurgeon, Charles - *Spiritual Parenting*

Holiness
Baxter, J. Sidlow - *A New Call to Holiness*
Blackaby, Henry T. - *Called and Accountable*
Blackaby, Henry & Blackaby, Richard - *God's Invitation: A Challenge to College Students*
Blackaby, Henry T. - *Lift High the Torch*

Bunyan, John - *A Holy Life*
Bunyan, John - *The Fear of God*
Chambers, Oswald - *Approved Unto God*
Chambers, Oswald - *My Utmost for His Highest*
Hession, Roy - *When I Saw Him*
McConkey, James - *The Surrendered Life*
Murray, Andrew - *Absolute Surrender*
Packer, J. I. - *A Quest for Godliness*
Ryle, J. C. - *Holiness*
Steinberger, G. - *In the Footprints of the Lamb*
Tozer, A.W. - *Knowledge of the Holy*

Holy Spirit

Chadwick, Samuel - *The Way to Pentecost*
Conner, Walter - *The Work of the Holy Spirit*
Goforth, Jonathan - *By My Spirit*
Herring, Ralph - *God Being My Helper*
Howard, David M. - *By the Power of the Holy Spirit*
Leavell, Landrum - *The Doctrine of the Holy Spirit*
Lawrence, J. B. - *The Holy Spirit and Missions*
McConkey, James - *The Threefold Secret of the Holy Spirit*
McQuilkin, J. Robertson - *Life in the Spirit*
Murray, Andrew - *The Spirit of Christ*
Sanders, J. Oswald - *The Holy Spirit and His Gifts*
Spurgeon, Charles - *The Holy Spirit's Power*
Stewart, James A. - *Heaven's Throne Gift*

Intercessory Prayer

Grubb, Norman - *Reese Howells: Intercessor*
Huegel, F. J. - *The Ministry of Intercession*
Hunt, T.W. - *The Doctrine of Prayer*
McClure, James - *Intercessory Prayer*
Moody, D. L. - *Prevailing Prayer*
Murray, Andrew - *Ministry of Intercessory Prayer*
Murray, Andrew - *With Christ in the School of Prayer*

Chapter 7
Personal Growth Library

Benjamin Warfield (CLASSIC)
The Inspiration and Authority of the Bible
B.B. Warfield is counted among the great theologians of the 19th century. He approached the Scriptures as authoritative and this volume is a collection of his writings on this topic of Biblical authority, useful for all who wish to defend the Scriptures in a modern, critical world.

Rick Warren
The Purpose Driven Life
Why am I here? What is my purpose? These are the most basic questions we face in life. Self-help books suggest that people should look within, at their own desires and dreams, but Rick Warren says the starting place must be with God and his eternal purposes for each life. Real meaning and significance comes from understanding and fulfilling God's purposes for putting us on earth.

Thomas Watson (CLASSIC)
All Things for Good
When Watson, along with two thousand other ministers, was ejected from the church of England and exposed to hardship and suffering, he wrote this inspiring testimony of Romans 8:28 and God's ability to "work all things together for good."

Robin Lee Hatcher

Best-selling novelist Robin Lee Hatcher whose many awards include the Christy Award for Excellence in Christian Fiction, the RITA Award for Best Inspirational, and RWA's Lifetime Achievement Award, is the author of over 40 contemporary and historical novels and novellas. There are nearly six million copies of her books in print in 14 countries. A frequent speaker to writers' and women's groups, Robin is a past president of Romance Writers of America, Inc., a professional writers' organization with more than 8,400 members worldwide. In recognition of her efforts on behalf of literacy, Laubach Literacy International (now known as ProLiteracy Worldwide) named The Robin Award in her honor.

What 5 books (other than the Bible) have had the largest impact on your life?

- *Redeeming Love* by Francine Rivers
- *The Hiding Place* by Corrie Ten Boom
- *Prison to Praise* by Merlin Carruthers
- *Experiencing God* by Henry Blackaby
- *Purpose Driven Life* by Rick Warren

What are you currently reading?

- **Bible Doctrine* by Wayne Grudem
- *Heaven* by Randy Alcorn
- *To Kill a Mockingbird* by Harper Lee

Thomas Watson (CLASSIC)
Doctrine of Repentance
Thomas Watson does not mince words: "Persons are veiled over with ignorance and self-love...The devil does with them as the falconer with the hawk. He blinds them and carries them hooded to hell." Repentance is essential to true Christianity and no better guide on the subject can be found.

John Wesley (CLASSIC)
The Holy Spirit and Power
Prepare for ten Spirit-empowered, original sermons of John Wesley. Not only that, this marvelous volume contains parts of Wesley's testimony, material from his journal, power points on the Holy Spirit at the end of each message and more.

George Whitefield (CLASSIC)
George Whitefield's Journals
In a time of crippling spiritual conditions in England, young George Whitefield preached his first sermon at age 22. Within weeks the crowds overflowed as he preached in England and America in the Great Awakening, a movement of such breadth and impact, there has been none quite like it since.

Warren Wiersbe (CLASSIC)
Best of A. W. Tozer Volume #1
These 52 favorite chapters compiled by Warren Wiersbe represent the major themes from Tozer's works, each one inspiring reflection and meditation.

Warren Wiersbe (CLASSIC)
Best of A. W. Tozer Volume #2
This is an outstanding collection of favorite passages from Tozer's most popular books. Says Warren Wiersbe, "Tozer walked with God and knew Him intimately." From his knowledge and pursuit of God come these excerpts of laser light to penetrate and illuminate the human heart.

David Wilkerson
The Cross and the Switchblade
When a young preacher left the hills of Pennsylvania to come to New York City, little did the world know he was an arrow sent from God to pierce the hearts of New York teens trapped by drugs and gangs. Over 14 million copies of David Wilkerson's amazing story are in print. Make sure you own one of them!

Dallas Willard
Renovation of the Heart
Dallas Willard addresses a critical question for today: Why are there so many Christians not growing closer to Christ-likeness and still struggling with sinful strongholds? *Renovation of the Heart* establishes a foundational understanding of human nature and the process of bringing about change.

Dallas Willard
Spirit of the Disciplines
One of today's most brilliant Christian minds explains how practice of the spiritual disciplines will enable ordinary men and women to enjoy the fruit of the Christian life. It is the key to self-transformation for everyone who wants to be a disciple of Jesus.

Dallas Willard
The Divine Conspiracy
This renowned teacher and writer calls us back to the true meaning of Christian discipleship. Willard argues compellingly for the relevance of God to every aspect of our existence, showing the necessity of profound changes in how we view our lives and faith.

Phillip Yancey
The Jesus I Never Knew
Philip Yancey reveals the real Jesus beyond the stereotypes, offering a new and different perspective on His life and work and ultimately, who He was and why He came. In this steady look at Christ's radical words, the author asks whether we are taking Jesus seriously enough.

John Ortberg

John Ortberg is a teaching pastor at Menlo Park Presbyterian Church in Menlo Park, California, and previously served as teaching pastor at Willow Creek Community Church. He is the best-selling author of *Everybody's Normal Till You Get to Know Them, If You Want to Walk on Water, You've Got to Get Out of the Boat, Love Beyond Reason, Old Testament Challenge* and many other titles. He has written for *Christianity Today* and is a frequent contributor to *Leadership Journal.*

What 5 books (other than the Bible) have had the largest impact on your life?

- *The Spirit of the Disciplines* by Dallas Willard—easily the most life-impacting book I've ever read.
- *The Divine Conspiracy* by Dallas Willard
- *Mere Christianity* by C.S. Lewis
- *Prince of Tides* by Pat Conroy (my favorite contemporary novel—Pat Conroy makes me want to write)
- *The Practice of the Presence of God* by Brother Lawrence

Philip Yancey

Philip Yancey serves as editor-at-large for *Christianity Today* magazine. He currently has more than 13 million books in print, including 12 Gold Medallion Award-winners and two, *What's So Amazing About Grace?* and *The Jesus I Never Knew*, that were awarded the Christian Book of the Year.

What 5 books (other than the Bible) have had the largest impact on your life?

- *Orthodoxy* by G.K. Chesterton truly brought me back to faith.
- *The Problem of Pain* by C.S. Lewis encouraged me to explore answers to my own questions on suffering.
- *Pilgrim at Tinker Creek* by Annie Dillard reconnected me to the natural world as a window to the Creator.
- *Brother to a Dragonfly* by Will Campbell got me thinking about my Southern childhood and about grace.
- *Telling the Truth* by Frederick Buechner raised my sights on what writing can do.

What got you into writing and what now are your goals as an author?

"I was attending grad school at Wheaton College and pounding doors of the Christian organizations located there until Harold Myra gave me a chance as a cub reporter at Campus Life. I worked there ten years, learning to write on the job and then went freelance. I'll always be grateful that I started writing for young people, a most fickle readership. I never had a 'captive' audience and that's a good discipline.

I think more in terms of my calling as an author than my goals. My calling is to represent the ordinary pilgrim encountering things like suffering, doubt, prayer, Jesus, spiritual growth, missions—and somehow coming to terms with them. I feel like an advocate, able to spend the time and reflection on these issues on behalf of my readers."

Phillip Yancey
What's So Amazing About Grace
"If grace is God's love for the undeserving," asks Yancey, "then how are believers doing at lavishing grace on a world that knows far more of cruelty and unforgiveness than it does of mercy?" Through powerful stories, Yancey takes a probing look at what grace looks like in action.

Phillip Yancey
Where is God When it Hurts
Winner of the Gold Medallion Award and an inspirational bestseller for more than twenty years, this is now revised and updated to explore issues that have arisen during that time. With sensitivity and caring, Yancey helps us understand why we suffer and how to cope with our own pain and that of others.

Ravi Zacharias
Can Man Live Without God
In this brilliant and compelling defense of the Christian faith, Ravi Zacharias shows that how you answer questions about God's existence will impact your relationship with others, your commitment to integrity, your attitude toward morality and your perception of truth.

Ravi Zacharias
Jesus Among Other Gods
Apologetics scholar and popular speaker Ravi Zacharias contrasts the truth of Jesus with founders of Islam, Hinduism and Buddhism, compelling believers to share their faith with our post-modern world. He shows how the blueprint for life and death itself is found in a true understanding of Jesus and celebrates the power of Jesus Christ to transform lives.

Footnotes

Note 1. Jerry Bridges, The Practice of Godliness (Colorado Springs, CO: Navpress, 1983, 1996), page 156.

Note 2. Robert C. Coleman, The Master Plan of Evangelism (Grand Rapids, Michigan: Fleming H. Revell Company, 1963,1964), page 38.

Note 3. Reprinted by permission of Thomas Nelson Inc., Nashville, TN., from the book entitled The Journey of Desire copyright date 2000 by John Eldredge. All rights reserved.

Note 4. Hannah Hurnard, Hinds Feet on High Places (Wheaton, Illinois: Living Books, Tyndale House Publishers, Inc.1975), page 241.

Note 5. Taken from: The Power of a Praying Wife. Copyright © 1997 by Stormie Omartian. Published by Harvest House Publishers, Eugene, Oregon. Used by permission.

Note 6. J.I. Packer, Knowing God (Downers Grove, Illinois: InterVarsity Press,1973), page 32.

Note 7. Hannah Whithall Smith, The Christian's Secret of a Happy Life (Old Tappan, New Jersey: Spire Books,1942), page 87.

Note 8. Charles Haddon Spurgeon, Morning and Evening (Hendrickson Publishers,1995), page 586.

Chapter 8
Personal Growth Library List by Category

Apologetics

Lewis, C.S., *Mere Christianity*
Little, Paul E., *Know What You Believe*
McDowell, Josh, *More than a Carpenter*
McDowell, Josh, *A Ready Defense*
Strobel, Lee, *Case for Faith*
Strobel, Lee, *Case for Christ*
Strobel, Lee, *Case for a Creator*
Zacharias, Ravi, *Jesus Among Other Gods*
Zacharias, Ravi, *Can Man Live Without God*

Biblical Studies

Blackaby, Henry, *Experiencing God*
Chafer, Lewis S, *Major Bible Themes*
Redpath, Alan, *Victorious Christian Life*
Schaeffer, Francis, *25 Basic Bible Studies*
Sproul, R.C., *What's in the Bible*
Watson, Thomas, *All Things for Good*

Biography/Biographical

Brother Andrew, *God's Smuggler*
Elliott, Elisabeth, *Shadow of the Almighty*
Elliott, Elisabeth, *Through the Gates of Splendor*

Foxe, John, *The New Foxes Book of Martyrs*
Lawson, *Deeper Experiences of Famous Christians*
Lewis, C.S., *Surprised By Joy*
McCasland, David, *Oswald Chambers: Abandoned to God*
Murray, Iain, *Jonathan Edwards: A New Biography*
Murray, Iain, *David Martyn Lloyd-Jones*
    the First Forty Years 1899-1939
Murray, Iain, *David Martyn Lloyd-Jones:*
    The Fight of Faith 1939-1981
Packer, J.I., *Faithfulness and Holiness:*
    The Witness of J.C. Ryle
Richardson, Don, *Peace Child*
Steer, George, *George Mueller: Delighted in God*
Tada, Joni Eareckson, *Joni - An Unforgettable Story*
Ten Boom, Corrie, *The Hiding Place 25th Anniversary Edition*
Wilkerson, David, *The Cross and the Switchblade*

Christian Classics

Thomas á Kempis, *Thomas, Imitation of Christ*
Bounds, Edward M., *Guide to Spiritual Warfare*
Drummond, Henry, *Greatest Things in the World*
Edwards, Jonathan, *Sinners in the Hands of an Angry God*
Edwards, Jonathan, *Religious Affections*
Edwards, Jonathan, *Works Of Jonathan Edwards Vol 1*
Edwards, Jonathan, *Works of Jonathan Edwards Vol 2*
Fenelon, *Talking with God*
Fenelon, *The Seeking Heart*
Foxe, John, *Foxes Book of Martyrs*
Gurnall, William, *Christian in Complete Armour 3 Vol Set*
Guyon, Jeanne, *Experiencing the Depths of Jesus Christ*
Lawrence, Brother, *The Practice of the Presence of God*
Luther, Martin, *Luther's Small Catechism*
Marshall, Peter, *Light and the Glory*
Murray, Andrew, *Abide in Christ*
Murray, Andrew, *Humility*
Murray, Andrew, *With Christ in the School of Prayer*
Murray, Andrew, *God's Best Secrets*
Ryle, J.C., *Holiness*

Sanders, J. Oswald, *Spiritual Leadership*
Sheldon, Charles, *In His Steps*
Smith, Hannah Whithall, *A Christian's Secret to a Happy Life*
Spurgeon, Charles Haddon, *Spurgeon on Prayer & Spiritual Warfare*
Spurgeon, Charles Haddon, *Holy Spirit Power*
Spurgeon, Charles Haddon, *Treasury of David*
St. Augustine, *Confessions*
St. Augustine, *City of God*
Tozer, A.W., *The Knowledge of the Holy*
Wesley, John, *The Holy Spirit and Power*
Whitefield, George, *George Whitefield's Journals*
Wiersbe, Warren, *Best of A. W. Tozer Volume #1*
Wiersbe, Warren, *Best of A. W. Tozer Volume #2*

Christian Living

Briner, Bob, *Roaring Lambs*
Chapman, Gary, *Five Love Languages*
Cloud, Henry, *Boundaries*
Colson, Charles, *How Now Shall We Live?*
Cymbala, Jim, *Fresh Wind, Fresh Fire*
Eldredge, John, *Wild at Heart*
Eldredge, John, *The Journey of Desire*
Elliott, Elisabeth, *Passion and Purity*
George, Elizabeth, *A Woman After God's Own Heart*
Graham, Billy, *Peace With God*
Hughes, R. Kent, *Disciplines of a Godly Man*
Hummel, Charles, *Tyranny of the Urgent*
Hybels, Bill, *Becoming a Contagious Christian*
Keller, W. Phillip, *Shepherd Looks at Psalm 23*
Lewis, C.S., *Weight of Glory*
Lewis, C.S., *Great Divorce*
Lewis, C.S., *Miracles*
Lewis, C.S., *Abolition of Man*
Lotz, Anne Graham, *Just Give Me Jesus*
Lucado, Max, *Just Like Jesus*
Lucado, Max, *No Wonder They Call Him Savior*

Lucado, Max, *In the Grip of Grace*
Lucado, Max, *Six Hours One Friday*
Manning, Brennen, *Ragamuffin Gospel*
McGee, Robert, *The Search for Significance*
Phillips, J.B., *Your God is Too Small*
Piper, John, *Don't Waste Your Life*
Piper, John, *Desiring God*
Ravenhill, Leon, *Why Revival Tarries*
Swenson, Richard, *Margin*
Swindoll, Charles R., *Intimacy with the Almighty*
Warren, Rick, *The Purpose Driven Life*
Willard, Dallas, *Renovation of the Heart*
Yancey, Phillip, *What's So Amazing About Grace*
Yancey, Phillip, *Jesus I Never Knew*

Church History

Eusebius, *Penguin Classics: The History of the Church from Christ to Constantine*
Shelley, Bruce, *Church History in Plain Language*

Church Life

Strauch, Alexander, *Biblical Eldership*

Devotionals

Bagster, Samuel, *Daily Light*
Chambers, Oswald, *My Utmost for His Highest*
Cowman, L.B., *Streams in the Desert*
Foster, Richard, *Devotional Classics*
Lucado, Max, *Grace for the Moment*
Murray, Andrew, *Absolute Surrender*
Roberts, Frances, *Come Away My Beloved*
Spurgeon, Charles Haddon, *Morning and Evening*

Evangelism

Coleman, Robert, *The Master Plan of Evangelism*

Fiction

Bunyan, John, *Pilgrims Progress*
Hurnard, Hannah, *Hinds Feet on High Places*
Lewis, C.S., *The Chronicles of Narnia (boxed edition)*
Lewis, C.S., *Till We Have Faces*

Lewis, C.S., *Screwtape Letters*
Lewis, C.S., *Space Trilogy*
Oursler, Fulton, *Greatest Story Ever Told*

Grief and Suffering

Lewis, C.S., *Problem of Pain*
Lewis, C.S., *Grief Observed*
Yancey, Phillip, *Where is God When it Hurts*

Life & Teachings of Jesus

Lloyd-Jones, Martin, *Studies on The Sermon on the Mount*
Stott, John R., *The Cross of Christ*

Other Religions

Martin, Walter, *The Kingdom of the Cults*
Ridenour, Fritz, *So What's the Difference*

Parenting

Dobson, Dr. James, *Parenting Isn't For Cowards*
Dobson, Dr. James, *Bringing Up Boys*
Dobson, Dr. James, *The New Dare to Discipline*
Dobson, Dr. James, *The New Strong-Willed Child*

Prayer

Bounds, Edward M., *Power Through Prayer*
Christenson, Evelyn, *What Happens When Women Pray*
Hybels, Bill, *Too Busy Not to Pray*
Omartian, Stormie, *The Power of a Praying Wife*
Sheets, Dutch, *Intercessory Prayer*

Spirituality

Bonhoeffer, Dietrick, *The Cost of Discipleship*
Bridges, Jerry, *Practice of Godliness*
Bridges, Jerry, *Trusting God*
Bridges, Jerry, *The Pursuit of Holiness*
Bridges, Jerry, *Discipline of Grace*
Carmichael, Amy, *If*
Colson, Charles, *Loving God*
Eldredge, John, *The Sacred Romance*
Foster, Richard, *Celebration of Discipline*
Manning, Brennen, *Ruthless Trust*
Nee, Watchman, *Normal Christian Life*

Nouwen, Henri, *The Return of the Prodigal Son:
A Story of Homecoming*
Piper, John, *A Godward Life*
Schaeffer, Francis, *True Spirituality*
Schaeffer, Francis, *Mark of a Christian*
Taylor, Howard, *Hudson Taylor's Spiritual Secrets*
Thomas, W. Ian, *Saving Life of Christ*
Tozer, A.W., *Attributes of God*
Tozer, A.W., *The Pursuit of God*
Willard, Dallas, *The Divine Conspiracy*
Willard, Dallas, *Spirit of the Disciplines*

Theology

Alcorn, Randy, *Heaven*
Berkhof, Louis, *The History of Christian Doctrines*
Boice, James M., *Foundations of the Christian Faith*
Calvin, John, *Institutes of the Christian Religion*
Charnock, Stephen, *The Existence and Attributes of God*
Chesterton, G.K., *Orthodoxy*
Edwards, Jonathan, *Freedom of the Will*
Graham, Billy, *Angels*
Little, Paul E., *Know Why You Believe*
Luther, Martin, *Bondage of the Will*
Packer, J.I., *Knowing God*
Pink, Arthur W., *Sovereignty of God*
Pink, Arthur W., *Attributes of God*
Ryrie, Charles, *Basic Theology*
Schaeffer, Francis, *He is There and Is Not Silent*
Schaeffer, Francis, *How Should We Then Live?*
Schaeffer, Francis, *Escape From Reason*
Schaeffer, Francis, *The God Who is There*
Sproul, R.C., *Chosen by God*
Sproul, R.C., *The Holiness of God*
Sproul, R.C., *Essential Truths of the Christian Faith*
Stott, John R., *Basic Christianity*
Warfield, Benjamin, *The Inspiration and Authority of the Bible*
Watson, Thomas, *Doctrine of Repentance*

Chapter 9
Life Issues Topical Resource List

What is a Life Issues Topical Resource List?

A friend at work says she's thinking about getting an abortion. Is there a book to help me talk with her?"

"My child is struggling with pornography. How can I help him?

"My sister wants to find a husband so badly. I just don't know what to say to her."

Where do you look for help when confronted with these types of difficult situations? The Life Issues Topical Resource List is your guide to highly recommended resources that will help you find answers. Grouped by the needs most often mentioned by Christian retailers throughout the country, we believe these books change lives.

Abortion

Beyond Regret: Entering into Healing and Wholeness After an Abortion (Video/Book) (Stephen Arterburn)

Empty Arms: Remembering the Unborn (Wendy Williams)

Forgiven and Set Free (Linda Cochrane)

Gianna: Aborted and Lived to Tell About It (Jessica Shaver)

Her Choice to Heal: Finding Spiritual and Emotional Peace After Abortion (Sydna Masse)

Pro-Life Answers to Pro-Choice Arguments (Randy Alcorn)

Solitary Sorrow (Teri and Paul Reisser)

Tilly (Frank Peretti)

Why Pro-Life? Caring for the Unborn and Their Mothers (Randy Alcorn)

You're Not Alone: Healing Through God's Grace After Abortion (Jennifer O'Neil)

Abortion, Men

Healing a Fathers Heart: A Post-Abortion Bible Study for Men (Linda Cochrane)

Abstinence/Purity

And the Bride Wore White (Dannah Gresh)

Come Clean (Doug Herman)

Every Young Man's Battle: Strategies for Victory in the Real World of Sexual Temptation (Stephen Arterburn)

Every Young Woman's Battle (Shannon Ethridge)

Gift Wrapped by God (Linda Dillow)

Keeping Your Kids Sexually Pure: A How-To Guide for Parents, Youth Workers and Teachers (LaVerne Tolbert)

Not Even a Hint (Joshua Harris)

Passion and Purity (Elisabeth Elliott)

Passport to Purity; Guide Your Child on an Adventure to

CHAPTER 8

Maturity (Dennis and Barbara Rainey)

Purity Under Pressure (Neil T. Anderson)

Quest for Love (Elisabeth Elliott)

Secret Keeper: The Delicate Power of Modesty (Dannah Gresh)

Sex Has a Price Tag (Pam Stenzel)

Teaching True Love to a Sex-at-13 Generation (Eric and Leslie Ludy)

The Love Killer: Answering Why True Love Waits (Josh McDowell)

The Naked Truth (Bill Perkins)

The Truth About Sex (Kay Arthur)

Wait for Me: The Beauty of Sexual Purity (Rebecca St. James)

Why True Love Waits: A Definitive Book on How to Help Your Youth Resist Sexual Pressure (Josh McDowell)

Abuse

Mending the Soul: Understanding and Healing Abuse (Steven Tracy)

Set Free: Stories of God's Healing Power for Abuse (Jan Coates)

Stumbling Toward Faith (Youth Specialties)

Abuse, Child

Caring for Sexually Abused Children: A Handbook for Families & Churches (Timothy Kearny)

Lord I Want To Be Whole: The Power of Prayer and Scripture in Emotional Healing (Stormie Omartian)

Abuse, Emotional

Healing the Scars of Emotional Abuse (Dr. Gregory L. Jantz)

Abuse, Sexual

A Safe Place (Jan Morrison)

Healing from Sexual Abuse (Kathleen)

Learning to Trust Again: A Young Woman's Journey to Healing From Sexual Abuse (Crista Sands)

Strength in Weakness: Overcoming Sexual and Relational Brokenness (Andrew Comisky)

The Wounded Heart: Hope for Adult Victims of Childhood Sexual Abuse (Dan Allender)

Abuse, Women

Angry Men and the Women Who Love Them: Breaking The Cycle of Physical and Emotional Abuse (Paul Hegstrom)

Dangerous Dating: Helping Young Women Break Out of Abusive Relationships (Patricia Gaddis)

No Place for Abuse: Biblical & Practical Resources (Catherine Kroeger)

Refuge from Abuse: Healing and Hope for Abused Christian Women (Nancy Nason-Clark)

Addictions

Good News For The Chemically Dependent and Those Who Love Them (Jeff Van Vonderen)

Overcoming Addictive Behavior (Neil Anderson)

Walking in Freedom: A 21 Day Devotional to Help Establish Your Freedom in Christ (Neil Anderson)

Addictions, Alcohol

Dying for a Drink (Alexander Dejong)

Freedom from Addiction (Neil Anderson)

God is for the Alcoholic (Jerry Dunn)

Seven Snares of the Enemy (Edwin Lutzer)

Addictions, Drug

More Than I Could Ever Ask (Lori Graham Bakker)

Tough Love (Pauline Neff)

Addictions, Gambling

Gambling Addiction: The Problem, the Pain and the Path to Recovery (John Eades)

Gambling: Don't Bet On It (Rex M. Rogers)

Tony Evans Speaks Out on Gambling and the Lottery (Tony Evans)

Turning the Tables on Gambling (Dr. Gregory L. Jantz)

Addictions, Pornography

Setting Captives Free: Pure Freedom: Breaking the Addiction to Pornography (Mike Cleveland)

The Pornography Trap (Ralph Earle)

The Silent War (Norm Miller)

Think Before You Look: 40 Powerful Reasons to Avoid Pornography (Daniel Henderson)

Addictions, Recovery/12 Steps

Celebrate Recovery (How to Set up a Recovery Program in Your Church) (Rick Warren)

Recovery Devotional Bible, NIV

Serenity New Testament and Psalms and Proverbs (NKJV)

The 12 Steps for Christians (Friends in Recovery)

The Twelve Step Life Recovery Devotional (Stephen Arterburn)

Addictions, Sexual

A Way of Escape: Freedom from Sexual Strongholds (Neil Anderson)

Breaking Free: Understanding Sexual Addiction and the Healing Power of Jesus (Bob Davies)

Every Heart Restored (Stephen Arterburn)

Fatal Attraction (Jack Hayford)

Healing The Wounds of Sexual Addiction (Dr. Mark Laaser)

Out of the Depths of Sexual Sin (Steve Gallagher)

Pure Desire: Helping People Break Free from Sexual Addictions (Jack W. Hayford)

The War Within (Robert Daniels)

Addictions, Smoking

Holy Smokes (Jean Glick)

Adoption

Adopting for Good (Jorie Kincaid)

Adopting The Hurt Child (Gregory C. Keck)

Loved by Choice (Susan Horner)

Parenting the Hurt Child (Gregory C. Keck)

Real Parents, Real Children: Parenting the Adopted Child (Holly Van lden)

Strength of Mercy (Kay Arthur and Jan Beazely)

The Whole Life Adoption Book (Jane Schooler)

Twenty Life Transforming Choices Adoptees Need to Make (Sherrie Eldridge)

Adoption, Children

Adopted and Loved Forever (Annetta Dellinger)

Shaoey and Dot (Steven Curtis Chapman)

Aging

Aging Gracefully: Keeping the Joy in the Journey (David Petty)

Fabulous After 50: Finding Fulfillment for Tomorrow (Jane Rubietta)

It Ain't Over Till It's Over: A User's Guide for the Second Half of Life (William Diehl)

The Joys of Successful Aging: Finishing With Grace (George Sweeting)

You Only Die Once: Preparing for the End of Life with a Purpose and a Plan (Margie Jenkins)

Aging, Alzheimers

A Promise Kept (Robertson McQuilkin)

Alzheimers: Caring for Your Loved One, Caring for Yourself (Sharon Fish)

Into the Shadows: A Journey of Faith and Love into Alzheimer's (Robert DeHaan)

My Journey into Alzheimers's Disease (Robert Davis)

The Long Good Night (Daphne Simpkins)

Twilight Travels With Mother (Mary Ann Mayo)

When Alzheimer's Disease Strikes, Revised (Stephen Sapp)

Aging, Care for Elderly

Caring for Aging Parents: Straight Answers That Help You Serve Their Needs Without Ignoring Your Own (Richard Johnson)

Complete Guide to Caring for Aging Loved Ones: A Lifeline for Those Navigating the Practical, Emotional and Spiritual Aspects of Caregiving (Focus on the Family Physicians Resource)

Aging, Children

Gram's Song (Aaren Henley)

Aging, Mid Life

Cooking With Hot Flashes (Martha Bolton)

Didn't My Skin Used to Fit (Martha Bolton)

Growing Young: Embracing the Joy and Accepting the Challenges of Mid-Life (Lois Mowday Rabey)

Living Somewhere Between Estrogen and Death (Barbara Johnson)

Men in Mid-Life Crisis (Jim Conway)

Mid-Course Correction: Re-ordering Your Private World for the Second Half of Life (Gordon MacDonald)

Someday Heaven (Patrick Morley)

Aging, Retirement

The Afternoon of Life (Elyse Fitzpatrick)

The Burkett & Blue Definitive Guide to Securing Wealth to Last: Money Essentials for the Second Half of Life (Larry Burkett)

The Joys of Successful Aging: Finishing With Grace (George Sweeting)

Autism

Facing Autism: Giving Parents a Reason for Hope and Guidance for Help (Lynn Hamilton)

The ADHD Autism Connection (Diane Kennedy)

The Gift of Autism: The Unexpected Joy of Parenting a Challenging Child (Mary Sharp)

Caregiving

A Caregiver's Survival Guide: How to Stay Healthy When Your Loved One Is Sick (Kay Marshall Strom)

American Medical Association Guide to Home Caregiving (Angela Perry and the American Medical Association)

Bedside Manners: A Practical Guide To Visiting The Ill (Katie Maxwell)

Real Love for Real Life: The Art and Work of Caregiving (Andi Ashworth)

Character/Manners

A Child's Book of Character Building (Rebekah and Ron Coriell)

A Little Book of Manners (Emilie Barnes)

A Little Book of Manners for Boys (Emilie Barnes)

As Iron Sharpens Iron: Building Character in a Mentoring Relationship (Howard Hendricks)

Excuse Me!: A Book All About Manners (Catherine Drinkwater Better)

Manners Matter (Hermine Hartley)

Stories That Build Character—includes CD (Steven Elkins)

The Book of Virtues (William Bennett)

The Children's Book of Virtues (William Bennett)

The Children's Treasury of Virtues (William Bennett)

Wise Guys: A Guide to Building Godly Character in Boys (Carol and Dan Fiddler)

Church

Breaking the Bondage of Legalism (Neil Anderson)

Escape from Church, Inc., The Return of the Pastor-Shepherd (Glenn Wagner)

Safe Kids: Policies and Procedures for Protection (Blake Caldwell)

Church, Leadership

Biblical Eldership (Alexander Strauch)

Called to be God's Leader (Henry Blackaby)

Christ in Church Leadership: A Handbook for Elders and Pastors (Paul Winslow)

Color Outside the Lines: A Revolutionary Approach to Creative Leadership (Howard Hendricks)

Courageous Leadership (Bill Hybels)

Developing the Leader Within You (John C. Maxwell)

Elders and Leaders (Gene Getz)

Jesus On Leadership (Gene Wilkes)

Leadership by the Book: Tools to Transform Your Workplace (Kenneth Blanchard)

Leadership Lessons of Jesus (Bob Briner)

Less Is More Leadership: 8 Secrets on How to Lead (H. Dale Burke)

Married to a Pastor: A Guide for Pastoral Couples on Surviving the Ministry (H.B. London, Jr.)

Pastors at Greater Risk: Real Help for Pastors from Pastors Who Have Been There (H.B. London, Jr.)

Spiritual Leadership (Oswald Saunders)

Spiritual Leadership: Moving People to God's Agenda (Henry Blackaby)

The 21 Irrefutable Laws of Leadership (John C. Maxwell)

The Book on Leadership (John MacArthur)

The Next Generation Leader: Five Essentials for Those That Will Shape the Future (Andy Stanley)

Church, Ordinances

Baptism: The Believer's First Obedience (Larry Dyer)

Christian Baptism (John Murray)

Church, Ordinances/Communion

In Remembrance of Me: A Manual on Observing the Lord's Supper (Jim Henry)

Two-Minute Messages for Communion Celebrations (Jim Townsend)

Church, Ordinances/Infant Baptism

Infant Baptism (John Sartelle)

Church, Small Groups

Building a Church of Small Groups (Bill Donahue)

Growing People Through Small Groups (Daivd Stark)

How to Build a Small Group Ministry (Neil McBride)

Leading Life Changing Small Groups (Bill Donahue)

Leading Small Groups That Help People Grow (Henry Cloud)

Seeker Small Groups (Gary Poole)

Small Group Idea Book: Resources to Enrich Communication (Cindy Bunch)

Small Group Ministry in the 21st Century (M. Scott Boren)

Small Group Q's (Laurie Polich)

Small Group Strategies: Ideas & Activities for Developing Spiritual Growth in Your Students (Laurie Polich)

The Big Book of Small Groups (Jeffrey Arnold)

The Search to Belong: Rethinking Intimacy, Community and Small Groups (Joseph R. Myers)

The Seven Deadly Sins of Small Group Ministry (Bill Donahue)

The Small Group (Dale Galloway)

Church Conflict

Facing Messy Church Stuff (Kenneth Swetland)

Firestorm: Preventing and Overcoming Church Conflicts (James D. Kennedy)

Managing Church Conflict (David Kale)

Pastors in Pain: How to Grow in Times of Conflict (Gary Preston)

The Wounded Minister: Healing from and Preventing Personal Attacks (Guy Greenfield)

Counseling

A Biblical Guide to Counseling the Sexual Addict (Steve Gallagher)

Christian Counseling: A Comprehensive Guide (Gary R. Collins)

The Christian Counselor's Manual (Jay Edward Adams)

Competent Christian Counseling (Timothy Clinton)

Competent to Counsel (Jay Edward Adams)

Help for Counselors: A Mini-Manual for Christian Counseling (Jay Edward Adams)

Hope When You're Hurting (Dr. Larry Crabb and Dr. Dan Allender)

Introduction To Biblical Counseling (John MacArthur, Jr.)

Quick Scripture Reference for Counseling (John Kruis)

Quick Scripture Reference for Counseling Women (Patricia Miller)

Resources for Christian Counseling: Counseling for Family Violence and Abuse (Grant Martin)

The Minirth Guide for Christian Counselors (Frank Minirth)

The New Guide to Crisis and Trauma Counseling (Norm Wright)

Dating/Singleness

10 Commandments of Dating (Ben Young)

Avoiding Mr. Wrong (And What To Do If You Didn't) (Stephen Arterburn)

Boundaries in Dating (Henry Cloud and John Townsend)

Boy Meets Girl (Joshua Harris)

Choosing God's Best (Don Rauniker)

Dateable: Are You? Are They? (Justin Lookadoo)

Define the Relationship (Jeramy Clark)

Don't Date Naked (Michael and Amy Smalley)

Ending the Search for Mr. Right (Michelle McKinney Hammond)

Finding Mr. Right and How To Know When You Have (Stephen Arterburn)

Finding the Love of Your Life: Ten Principles for Choosing the Right Marriage Partner (Neil Clark Warren)

Finding True Love: A Devotional Journal for Youth (Josh McDowell)

Finding Your Million Dollar Mate (Randy Pope)

Getting It Right: Going Out Without Freaking Out (Time Baker)

He's Hot, She's Hot: What to Look for in the Opposite Sex (Jeramy Clark)

How to Get a Date Worth Keeping (Dr. Henry Cloud)

I Gave Dating A Chance (Jeramy Clark)

I Kissed Dating Goodbye Updated (Joshua Harris)

If Men Are Like Buses Then How Do I Catch One? (Michelle McKinney Hammond)

If Singleness is a "Gift," What's the Return Policy? (Holly Virdon)

Lady in Waiting (Jackie Kendall and Debbie Jones)

Love Decisions (Dr. Donald Harvey)

The Dateable Rules (Justin Lookadoo)

The Dirt on Breaking Up (Justin Lookadoo)

The Dirt on Sex (Justin Lookadoo)

The Perfect Match: Finding and Keeping the Love of Your Life (Kevin Leman)

The Ten Commandments of Dating: Student Edition (Ben Young)

Time for a Pure Revolution (Doug Herman)

What to Do Until Love Finds You: Preparing Yourself for Your Perfect Mate (Michelle McKinney Hammond)

When God Writes Your Love Story (Eric and Leslie Ludy)

Your Single Treasure (Rick Stedman)

Divorce/Remarriage

A Passage Through Divorce: An Interactive Journal for Healing (Barbara Baumgardner)

A Woman's Guide to Healing the Heartbreak of Divorce (Rose Sweet)

Before You Remarry (Norm Wright)

Divorce-Proof Your Marriage (Gary and Barbara Rosberg)

Growing Through Divorce (Jim Smoke)

Happily Remarried: *Making Decisions Together *Blending Families Successfully *Building A Love That Will Last (David Frisbie)

Lifelines for Recovery Series: The Complete Divorce Recovery Handbook (John P. Splinter)

Love Busters: Overcoming Habits That Destroy Romantic Love (Willard Harley)

Love Lost: Living Beyond a Broken Marriage (Dr. David Hawkins)

Marriage, Divorce and Remarriage in the Bible (Jay Edward Adams)

Moving Forward: A Devotional Guide for Finding Hope and Peace in the Midst of Divorce (Jim Smoke)

New Life After Divorce (Bill Butterworth)

The Blended Marriage (Gary Smalley)

When Love Dies: How to Save a Hopeless Marriage (Judy Bodmer)

Winning Your Husband Back Before It's Too Late: Whether He's Left Physically or Emotionally, All That Matters Is.. (Gary Smalley)

Winning Your Wife Back Before It's Too Late: Whether She's Left Physically or Emotionally, All That Matters Is...(Gary Smalley)

Divorce/Remarriage, Blended Families

Blended Families: Creating Harmony as You Build a New Home Life (Maxine Marsolini)

Daily Reflections for Stepparents (Margaret Broersma)

I'm Not Your Kid: A Christian's Guide to a Healthy Stepfamily (Kay Adkins)

Living in a Step-family Without Getting Stepped On: Helping Your Children Survive The Birth Order Blender (Kevin Leman)

Seven Keys to a Healthy Blended Family (Jim Smoke)

Stepparent to Stepparent (Margaret Broersma)

The Savvy Couple's Guide to Marrying after 35 (Kay Marshall Strom)

The Smart Stepfamily (Ron Deal)

Tying the Family Knot (Terri Clark)

You're Not My Mom: Confessions of a Formerly "Wicked" Stepmother (Kate and Elizabeth Schieders)

Divorce/Remarriage, Children
With My Mom, With My Dad: a Book About Divorce (Maribet Boelts)

Divorce/Remarriage, Children of Divorce
Children and Divorce: What to Expect, How to Help (Archibald Hart)

Children of Divorce (Debbie Barr-Stewart)

What Children Need to Know When Parents Get Divorced (William Coleman)

Your Kids and Divorce: Helping Them Grow Beyond the Hurt (Tom Whiteman)

Divorce/Remarriage, Separation
Hope for the Separated (Revised and Updated) (Gary Chapman)

Divorce/Remarriage, Single Again
Making a New Vow: A Christian's Guide to Remarrying After Divorce (Joseph Kniskern)

Divorce/Remarriage, Teen
Friendship 911 Collection: My Friend is Struggling With Divorce of Parents (Josh McDowell)

Eating Disorders
Breaking Free from Anorexia & Bulimia (Dr. Linda Mintle)

Diary of an Anorexic Girl (Morgan Menzie)

Getting Unstuck: Clear Answers for Women on Why We Get Trapped in Depression, Anxiety and Eating Disorders (Dr. Linda Mintle)

Hope, Help and Healing for Eating Disorders: A New Approach to Treating Anorexia, Bulimia and Overeating (Dr. Gregory L. Jantz)

Love to Eat, Hate to Eat: Breaking The Bondage of Destructive Eating Habits (Elyse Fitzpatrick)

Mercy for Eating Disorders (Nancy Alcorn)

Releases From Bondage (Neil Anderson)

The Monster Within: Facing an Eating Disorder (Cynthia Rowland McClure)

The Pursuit of Beauty: Finding True Beauty That Will Last Forever (Katie Luce)

Emotional Needs

Boundaries (Henry Cloud)

Boundaries Workbook (Henry Cloud)

Changes That Heal (Henry Cloud)

Deadly Emotions (Don Colbert)

Feeding Your Appetites: Take Control of What's Controlling You! (Stephen Arterburn)

Healing for Damaged Emotions (Davids A. Seamands)

Healing for Damaged Emotions Workbook (Davids A. Seamands)

Hope Rising (Kim Meeder)

In Pursuit of Happiness: Choices That Can Change Your Life (Frank Minirth)

Letting God Meet Your Emotional Needs (Cindi McMenaman)

Making Peace With Your Father (Dr. David Stoop)

The Obsessive-Compulsive Trap (Dr. Mark Crawford)

Wounds that Heal (Stephen Seamands)

Emotional Needs, ADD/ADHD

A.D.H.D. Attention Deficit Hyperactivity Disorder: A Natural Approach to Help and Heal a Hyperactive Child (Ted Broer)

Adult AD/HD: A Reader Friendly Guide to Identifying, Understanding and Treating Adult Attention Deficit/Hyperactivity Disorder (Michele Novotni)

Give Your ADD Teen a Chance: A Guide for Parents of Teenagers with Attention Deficit Disorder (Lynn Weiss)

Honey Are You Listening? Attention Deficit/Hyperactivity Disorder and Your Marriage (Rick and Jerilyn Fowler)

Real Solutions for Living with ADHD (John Timmerman)

The Link Between ADD and Addiction (Wendy Richardson)

When Too Much Isn't Enough: Ending the Destructive Cycle of AD/HD and Addictive Behavior (Wendy Richardson)

Why A.D.H.D. Doesn't Mean Disaster (Dennis Swanberg)

Emotional Needs, Anger

Getting the Best of Your Anger (Les Carter)

Letting Go of Anger and Frustration (Pam and John Vredevelt)

Making Anger Your Ally (Neil Clark Warren)

Overcoming Hurts and Anger (Dwight Carlson)

The Anger Trap: Free Yourself from the Frustrations That Sabotage Your Life (Dr. Les Carter)

The Anger Workbook (Les Carter)

Emotional Needs, Anger/Teens

The Angry Teenager: Why Teens Get So Angry and How Parents Can Help Them Grow Through It (William Lee Carter)

Angry Teens and the Parents Who Love Them (Sandra Austin)

Emotional Needs, Anger/Women

She's Gonna Blow (Julie Anne Barnhill)

Woman's Answer to Anger: Getting Your Emotions Under Control (Annie Chapman)

Emotional Needs, Anxiety

Finding Peace: Gods Promise of a Life Free from Regret Anxiety and Fear (Charles Stanley)

How to Win Over Worry (John Haggai)

Just Enough Light for the Step I'm On (Stormie Omartian)

Overcoming Anxiety (David Hazard)

Overcoming Fear, Worry and Anxiety: Becoming A Woman of Faith and Confidence (Elyse Ftizpatrick)

Partly Cloudy With Scattered Worries (Kathy Collard Miller)

The Anxiety Cure (Archibald Hart)

The Worry Workbook (Les Carter)

Emotional Needs, Depression

A Ladder Out of Depression (Bonnie Keen)

Breaking Free From Depression (Dr. Linda Mintle)

Coming Out of the Dark (Mary Sutherland)

Conquering Depression: A 30-Day Plan to Finding Happiness (Mark Sutton)

Does Your Man Have the Blues? (David Hawkins)

Finding Hope Again (Neil Anderson)

Getting Over the Blues (Leslie Vernick)

Happiness is a Choice (Frank Minirth)

Healthy Body, Healthy Soul: Breaking Free from Depression: Natural Remedies for Better Living (David Hazard)

How to Win Over Depression (Tim LaHaye)

Minirth Meier New Life Clinic Series: The Freedom from Depression Workbook (Les Carter)

Moving Beyond Depression: A Whole-Person Approach (Dr. Gregory Jantz, LL)

New Light on Depression: Help, Hope and Answers for the Depressed and Those Who Love Them (David Biebel)

Overcoming Depression (Neil Anderson)

Unmasking Male Depression (Archibald Hart)

Unveiling Depression in Women (Archibald Hart)

Victory Over Depression: Lasting Victory Over Disappointment and Depression (Bob George)

Emotional Needs, Fear

Be Not Afraid (David Ivaska)

Freedom from Fear (Neil Anderson)

Freedom From the Grip of Fear (Norm Wright)

Emotional Needs, Fear/Worry/Children

Am I Trusting? (Jeannie St. John Taylor)

Don't Cry Lion (Dandi Daley Mackall)

Don't Worry About Tomorrow (Melody Carlson)

Go, Go, Fish! (Dandi Daley Mackall)

No, No, Noah! (Dandi Daley Mackall)

Sometimes I'm Afraid (Maribet Boelts)

Where is God When I'm Scared (Cindy Kenney)

Emotional Needs, Mental Illnesses

When Your Family is Living with Mental Illness (Marcia Lund)

Emotional Needs, Stress

5-Minute Retreats for Women: Stress Proof Your Life (Sue Augustine)

Is There Life After Stress (James Moore)

Juggling Chainsaws on a Tightrope: On Stress (Navigators)

Just Hand Over the Chocolate and No One Will Get Hurt (Karen Linneman)

Living Above Worry and Stress (Thelma Wells)

Living in Harmony: Moving to a Better Place in Your Life (Richard Exley)

Margin: Restoring Emotional, Physical, Financial and Time Reserves to Overloaded Lives (Richard Swenson)

Say Goodbye to Stress (Kevin Leman)

Stress and the Woman's Body (David Hayer)

Stress Less (Don Colbert)

Women and Stress: A Practical Approach to Managing Tension (Jean Lush)

Emotional Needs, Stress/Families

Stress and Your Child (Archibald Hart)

Evangelism

101 Ways to Reach Your Community (Steve Sjogren)

Becoming a Contagious Christian: Communicating Your Faith in a Style That Fits You (Bo Boshers)

Evangelism Explosion 4th Edition (James D. Kennedy)

Evangelism Outside the Box: New Ways to Help People Experience the Good News (Rick Richardson)

Finding Common Ground (Tim Downs)

Going Public With Your Faith (William Peel)

How to Give Away Your Faith: With Study Questions for Individuals or Groups (Paul E. Little)

How to Lead a Seeker Bible Discussion (Rebecca Manley Pippert)

How to Share Your Faith (Greg Laurie)

I Believe in Jesus: Leading Your Child To Christ (John MacArthur)

Jesus Plan: Breaking Through Barriers to Introduce the People You Know to the God You Love (Bruce Robert Dreisbach)

Last Chance: A Student Survival Guide to End-Times Evangelism (Greg Stiers)

Lifeguide Bible Studies: Evangelism (Rebecca Pippert)

Lifestyle Evangelism (Joe Aldrich)

Looking at the Life of Jesus: 7 Seeker Bible Discussions in the Gospel of John (Rebecca Manley Pippert)

Out of the Saltshaker & Into the World: Evangelism As a Way of Life (Rebecca Manley Pippert)

Reaching the World in Our Own Backyard (Rajendra Pillai)

Sharing Jesus Without Fear (William Fay)

Sharing Your Faith With A Buddhist (Madasamy Thiramalai)

Sharing Your Faith With Friends and Family (Michael Green)

Talking About Jesus Without Sounding Religious (Rebecca Manley Pippert)

Telling the Truth: Evangelizing Postmoderns (D.A. Carson)

The Coffeehouse Gospel (Matthew Paul Turner)

The Way of Jesus (Rebecca Manley Pippert)

Fasting

7 Basic Steps to Successful Fasting & Prayer (Bill Bright)

A Hunger for God: Desiring God Through Fasting and Prayer (John Piper)

Fasting for Spiritual Breakthrough (Elmer Towns)

Let Prayer Change Your Life: Discover the Awesome Power of, Empowering Discipline of and Ultimate Design for Prayer (Becky Tirabassi)

The Beginners Guide to Fasting (Elmer Towns)

The Power of Prayer and Fasting: 10 Secrets of Spiritual Strength (Bill Bright)

Tony Evans Speaks Out on Fasting (Tony Evans)

Finding and Knowing God's Will

Affirming the Will of God (Paul Little)

Decision Making and the Will of God (Gary Friessen)

Decision Making God's Way: A New Model for Knowing God's Will (Gary Meadors)

Discovering God's Will for Your Life (Ray Pritchard)

Experiencing God: How to Live the Full Adventure of Knowing and Doing the Will of God (Henry Blackaby)

Finding and Following God's Will (Jane Kise)

Finding God's Will in Spiritually Deceptive Times (Neil Anderson)

Finding the Will of God in a Crazy, Mixed-Up World (Tim LaHaye)

Finding the Will of God: A Pagan Notion? (Bruce Waltke)

Five Steps to Knowing God's Will (Bill Bright)

Found God's Will (John MacArthur)

Hearing the Master's Voice: The Comfort and Confidence of Knowing God's Will (Robert Jeffries)

Knowing and Doing the Will of God (J.I. Packer)

Knowing God's Will Made Easier (Mark Water)

Listening to God in Times of Choice: The Art of Discerning God's Will (Gordon T. Smith)

Living the Life God Has Planned: A Guide to Knowing God's Will (Bill Thrasher)

Understanding God's Will: How to Hack the Equation Without Formulas (Kyle Lake)

The Call: Finding and Fulfilling the Central Purposes in Your Life (Os Guiness)

Grief

A Decembered Grief: Living With Loss While Others Are Celebrating (Harold Ivan Smith)

A Grace Disguised (Jerry Sittser)

A Grief Observed (C.S. Lewis)

A Hand to Hold: Helping Someone Through Grief (Lauraine Snelling)

Experiencing Grief (Norm Wright)

Good-Bye for Now: Practical Help and Personal Hope (Welby O'Brien)

Good Grief (Granger Westberg)

Grief Recovery Workbook: Helping You Weather the Storm of Loss and Overwhelming Disappointment (includes CD-ROM) (Ray Giunta)

Grieving the Loss of Someone You Love: Daily Meditations (Ray Mitsch)

Helping Those Who Hurt (Norm Wright)

How to Help a Grieving Friend (Stephanie Whitson)

Journaling Your Decembered Grief: To Help You Through Your Loss (Harold Ivan Smith)

Moments for Those That Have Lost a Loved One (Lois Mowday-Rabey)

Roses in December: Finding Strength Within Grief (Marilyn Heavilin)

Sunsets: Reflections for Life's Final Journey (Deborah Howard)

The Empty Chair: Handling Grief on Holidays and Special Occasions (Susan Zonnebelt-Smeenge)

The Light That Never Dies (William Hendricks)

The Reluctant Traveler: A Pilgrimage Through Loss and Recovery (Diane Dempsey Marr)

Through A Season of Grief (Bill Dunn)

When Will I Stop Hurting? Dealing With a Recent Death (June Cerza Kolf)

Grief, Children

Children and Grief: Helping Your Child Understand (Joey O'Connor)

Helping Children Grieve (Theresa Huntley)

If Nathan Were Here (Mary Bahr)

It's Okay to Cry: A Parent's Guide to Helping Children Through the Losses of Life (Norm Wright)

It's Okay to Cry (Norm Wright)

Never Say Goodbye (Lea Gillespie Gant)

Papa's Gift (Kathleen Bostrom)

Peekaboo, Pearly Moon (Karen DeVries)

Please Help Me God Series: Someone I Love Died (Christine Tangveld)

Sarah's Grandma Goes to Heaven: A Book About Grief (Maribet Boelts)

The Day Scooter Died: A Book About the Death of a Pet (Kathleen Bostrom)

The Goodbye Boat (Claire St. Louis Little)

The Wonderful Way Babies Are Made (Carolyn Nystrom)

Grief, Death of a Child

Mommy Please Don't Cry (Linda Deymaz)

Safe in the Arms of God: Words from Heaven about the Death of a Child (John MacArthur)

Trusting God Through Tears: A Story to Encourage (Jehu Thomas Burton and Dan Allender)

Grief, Death of a Father

A Thousand Goodbyes: A Son's Reflection on Living, Dying and the Things That Matter Most (Jim Huber)

When Your Father Dies: How a Man Deals With the Loss of His Father (David Veerman)

Grief, Death of a Son

Not by Accident: What I Learned from My Son's Untimely Death (Isabel Fleece)

Grief, Death of a Spouse

He Gathers Your Tears: Words of Comfort for a Widow's Heart (Phylis Moore)

Learning to Breathe Again (Tammy Trent)

Let Me Grieve, But Not Forever (Verdell Davis)

Living Fully in the Shadow of Death (Zonnebelt-Smeenge)

When Your Soul Aches: Hope and Help for Women Who Have Lost Their Husbands (Lois Mowday-Rabey)

Grief, Teen

The Grieving Teen: A Guide for Parents, Counselors and Teenagers (Helen Fitzgerald)

Saying Goodbye When You Don't Want To: Teens Dealing With Loss (Martha Bolton)

Health Issues

When Your Doctor Has Bad News: Simple Steps to Strength, Healing and Hope (Al Weir M.D.)

Health Issues, Cancer

A Journey Through Cancer: My Story of Hope, Healing and God's Amazing Faithfulness (Emilie Barnes)

Cancer: A Medical and Spiritual Guide for Patients (William A. Fintel M.D.)

Hope in the Face of Cancer: A Survival Guide for the Journey You Did Not Choose (Amy Givler)

Minute Meditations for Healing and Hope (Emilie Barnes)

Plant a Geranium in Your Cranium (Barbara Johnson)

The Word on the Street (Rob Lacey)

Health Issues, Cancer/Breast

A Spiritual Journey through Breast Cancer (Judy Asti)

Getting Better, Not Bitter: A Spiritual Prescription for Breast Cancer (Brenda Ladun)

Grace for Each Hour: Through the Breast Cancer Journey (Mary J. Nelson)

Stepping into the Ring (Nicole Johnson)

Thanks for the Mammogram! Fighting Cancer with Faith, Hope and a Healthy Dose of Laughter (Laura Jensen Walker)

When God & Cancer Meet (Lynn Eib)

The Breast Cancer Care Book: A Survival Guide for Patients and Loved Ones (Sally Knox)

Health Issues, Cancer/Child
Walking Taylor Home (Brian Schauger)

Health Issues, Cancer/Teen
Six Months to Live: Learning from a Young Man with Cancer (Daniel Hallock)

Health Issues, Disability
Sundays with Scottie (Milton Jones)

Health Issues, Menopause
Bible Cure: Menopause: Ancient Truths, Natural Remedies and the Latest Findings for Your Health Today (Don Colbert)

Mentalpause...and Other Mid-life Laughs (Laura Jensen Walker)

Postcards from Menopause, Wishing I Weren't Here (Lois Mowday Rabey)

Take Charge of the Change: Nourishing Your Body and Spirit-Now Through Menopause (Pamela Smith)

The Heat is On (Danna Demetre)

The Menopause Manager: A Safe Path for a Natural Change (Joseph and Mary Mayo)

Heaven/Hell

55 Answers to Questions about Life After Death (Mark Hitchcock)

Four Views On Hell (William Crockett)

Heaven (Randy Alcorn)

Heaven: My Father's House (Anne Graham Lotz)

Heaven or Hell (Bill Bright)

Heaven: Your Real Home (Joni Erickson Tada)

Heaven: Finding Our True Home (Douglas Connelly)

One Minute After You Die (Erwin Lutzer)

The Glory of Heaven (John MacArthur)

Tony Evans Speaks Out on Heaven and Hell (Tony Evans)

What Really Happens When You Die? (Ralph Muncaster)

Your Eternal Reward (Erwin Lutzer)

Heaven/Hell, Children

Grandpa, Is There a Heaven? (Katherine Bohlman)

Someday Heaven (Larry Libby)

What Happened When Grandma Died (Peggy Barker)

Holidays/Traditions

Beyond Groundhogs and Gobblers: Putting Meaning Back Into Your Holiday Celebrations (Cyndy Salzman)

Celebrating Special Times with Special People (Shirley Dobson and Gloria Gaither)

Celebrations That Touch the Heart: Creative Ideas to Make Your Holidays and Special Events Meaningful (Brenda Poinsett)

Family Night Tool Chest: Holiday Family Nights (Kurt Bruner)

Holidays and Holy Days: Origins, Customs and Perspectives on Celebrations Through the Year (Susan Richardson)

Holidays/Traditions, Children

Benjamin's Box (Melody Carlson)

Duncan Carries a King (Dan Taylor)

Halloween: Is it for Real? (Harold Myra)

Easter Bunny Are You for Real? (Harold Myra)

Off to Plymouth Rock (Dandi Daley Makall)

Squanto and the Miracle of Thanksgiving (Eric Metaxas)

Thanksgiving What Makes It Special? (Harold Myra)

The Tale of Three Trees (Angela Hunt)

When the Creepy Things Come Out (Melody Carlson)

Holidays/Traditions, Christmas

How Great Our Joy: Family Memories and Meditations for Christmas (Ray and Anne Ortlund)

Redeeming the Season: Simple Ideas for a Memorable and Meaningful Christmas (Kim Wier)

Holidays/Traditions, Christmas/Children

Annika's Secret Wish (Beverly Lewis)

Clopper the Christmas Donkey (Emily King)

If You're Missing Baby Jesus (Jeanne Jeffrey Gietzen)

Jotham's Journey (Arnold Ytreeide)

Legend of the Christmas Stocking: An Inspirational Story of a Wish Come True (Rick Osborne)

Silent Night: The Song and Its Story (Margaret Hodges)

That Blessed Christmas Night (Dori Chaconas)

That's Not All I Want for Christmas (Lynn Hodges)

The Candle in the Window: A Christmas Legend (Grace Johnson)

The Christmas Troll (Eugene Peterson)

The Crippled Lamb with DVD (Max Lucado)

The Legend of the Candy Cane (Rich Osborne)

The Star of Christmas (Cindy Kinney)

The Very First Christmas (Paul Maier)

Holidays/Traditions, Easter

Case for the Resurrection of Jesus (Gary R. Habermas and Michael R. Licona)

The Case for Easter (Lee Strobel)

The Passion of Jesus Christ (John Piper)

Why Celebrate Easter (Steve Russo)

Holidays/Traditions, Halloween

Halloween (Steve Russo)

Redeeming Halloween (Kim Wier)

The Facts on Halloween (John Ankerberg)

Holidays/Traditions, Messianic

God's Appointed Times: A Practical Guide for Understanding and Celebrating the Biblical Holidays (Barney Kasdan)

Infertility

Empty Womb, Aching Heart: Hope and Help for Those Struggling With Infertility (Marlo Schalesky)

Hannah's Hope: Seeking God's Heart in the Midst of Infertility, Miscarriage and Adoption Loss (Jennifer Saake)

Longing for a Child: Devotions of Hope for Your Journey (Kathe Wunnenberg)

Moments for Couples Who Long for Children (Ginger Garrett)

The Infertility Companion (William and Glahn Cutrer)

Water from the Rock: Finding God's Comfort in the Midst of Infertility (Donna Gibbs)

When Empty Arms Become a Heavy Burden: Encourage Me (Sandra Glahn)

When the Cradle is Empty (John and Sylvia Regenmorter)

When You are Coping with Infertility (Vera Snow)

Marriage

Boundaries in Marriage (Henry Cloud and John Townsend)

Boundaries in Marriage Workbook (Henry Cloud and John Townsend)

I, Isaac, Take Thee, Rebekah: Moving from Romance to Lasting Love (Ravi Zacharias)

Why Men and Women Act the Way They Do, The Reasons Might Surprise You (Bill and Pam Farrel)

Marriage, Conflict

Because I Said Forever: Embracing Hope in an Imperfect Marriage (Debbie Kalmbach)

Divorce-Proofing Your Marriage: 10 Lies That Lead to Divorce and 10 Truths That Will Stop It (Dr. Linda Mintle)

Dumb Things He Does/Dumb Things She Does: How To Stop Doing the Things That Drive Women/Men Crazy (Holly Wagner)

Fight Fair: Winning At Conflict Without Losing At Love (Tim Downs)

Healing the Hurt in Your Marriage (Gary and Barbara Rosberg)

How to Act Right When Your Spouse Acts Wrong (Leslie Vernick)

Love Busters: Overcoming Habits That Destroy Romantic Love (Willard Harley)

The Seven Conflicts: Resolving the Most Common Disagreements in Marriage (Tim Downs)

What Husbands and Wives Aren't Telling Each Other (Steve and Annie Chapman)

When Bad Things Happen to Good Marriages (Les Parrot)

Marriage, Infidelity

His Needs, Her Needs: Building an Affair-Proof Marriage (Willard Harley)

Surviving An Affair (Willard Harley)

The Dance of Restoration: Rebuilding Marriage After Infidelity (Abel Ortega and Melodie Fleming)

Torn Asunder (Dave Carder)

Marriage, Newlyweds

A Celebration of Sex for Newlyweds (Douglas Rosenau)

Getting Your Sex Life Off to a Great Start: A Guide for Engaged and Newlywed Couples (Clifford and Joyce Penner)

Great Expectations: An interactive Guide to Your First Year of Marriage (Toben and Joanne Heim)

Mentoring Engaged and Newlywed Couples Participant's Guide (Les Parrot)

Sex 101 (Clifford and Joyce Penner)

The New Bride Guide: Everything You Need to Know for the First Year of Marriage (Ellie Kay)

Marriage, Non-believing Spouse

Beloved Unbeliever (Jo Perry)

Between Two Loves (Nancy Kennedy)

Can Two Walk Together? Encouragement for Spiritually Unbalanced Marriages (Sabrina Black)

How to Pray When He Doesn't Believe (Maureen Tizzard)

Surviving a Spiritual Mismatch in Marriage (Lee Strobel)

When He Doesn't Believe: Help and Encouragement for Women Who Feel Alone in Their Faith (Nancy Kennedy)

Marriage, Pornography Within Marriage

An Affair of the Mind: One Woman's Courageous Battle to Salvage Her Family from the Devastation of Pornography (Laurie Sharlene Hall)

Living With Your Husband's Secret Wars (Marsha Means)

When His Secret Sin Breaks Your Heart (Kathy Gallagher)

Marriage, Pregnancy

An Expectant Mother's Journal (Angela Thomas Guffey)

Christian Family Guide to Pregnancy and Childbirth (Michelle Gliksman)

Dear Lord, I Feel Like a Whale: Knowing God's Touch (Jane Bullivant)

Healthy Expections: Preparing a Healthy Body for a Healthy Baby (Pamela Smith)

Love Letters to My Baby: A Guided Journal for Expectant and New Mothers (Vickey Banks)

The Christian Woman's Guide to Childbirth (Debra Evans)

We've Been Waiting for You (Carolyn Arrends)

When the Belly Button Pops, the Baby's Done: A Month-By-Month Guide to Surviving (and Loving) Your Pregnancy (Lorilee Craker)

You're Going to Be My Mom! A 40-Week Devotional (Rivera Astrid)

Marriage, Pregnancy/Children

Before You Were Born (Michael and Kelly Molinet)

God's Design for Sex: Before I Was Born (Carolyn Nystrom)

The Wonderful Way That Babies Are Made (Larry Christenson)

Marriage, Sexual Issues

A Celebration of Sex After 50 (Douglas Rosenau)

Intended for Pleasure (Ed Wheat)

Intimate Issues (Linda Dillow)

Love, Sex and Lasting Relationships (Chip Ingram)

Sacred Sex (Tim Alan Gardner)

Sex…According to God (Kay Arthur)

The Act of Marriage (Tim LaHaye)

The Act of Marriage After 40 (Tim LaHaye)

The Contraception Guidebook: Options, Risks and Answers for Christian Couples (Dr. William Cutrer)

The Gift of Sex (Clifford and Joyce Penner)

Men's Issues

At the Altar of Sexual Idolatry (Stephen Gallagher)

Being God's Man as a Satisfied Single (Stephen Arterburn)

Being God's Man by Pursuing Friendships (Stephen Arterburn)

Being God's Man in Leading a Family (Stephen Arterburn)

Being God's Man in the Face of Temptation (Stephen Arterburn)

Being God's Man in the Search for Success (Stephen Arterburn)

Being God's Man in Tough Times (Stephen Arterburn)

Dangers Men Face (Jerry White)

Every Man, God's Man (Stephen Arterburn)

Every Man's Battle Guide (Stephen Arterburn)

Every Man's Battle: Winning the War on Sexual Temptation One Victory at a Time (Stephen Arterburn)

Every Man's Challenge (Stephen Arterburn)

God's Gift to Women: Becoming the Man You Were Meant to Be (Eric Ludy)

Men's Secret Wars (Patrick Means)

Second Half of the Man in the Mirror (Patrick Morley)

Seven Seasons of the Man in the Mirror (Patrick Morley)

Sex and the Single Guy: Winning Your Battle for Purity (Joseph Knable)

Temptations Men Face: Straightforward Talk on Power, Money, Affairs, Perfectionism, Insensitivity (Tom Eisenman)

The Man in the Mirror (Patrick Morley)

Wild at Heart: Discovering the Secret of a Man's Soul (John Eldredge)

Men's Issues, Youth

Every Young Man's Battle Guide (Stephen Arterburn)

The Struggle (Steve Gerali)

The Young Man in the Mirror: A Rite of Passage into Manhood (Patrick Morley)

Miracles

A Treasury of Miracles for Women: True Stories of God's Presence Today (Karen Kingsbury)

It's A God Thing (Luis Palau)

Miracles (C.S. Lewis)

Unsolved Miracles (John Van Diest)

Miscarriage

Empty Arms: Hope and Support for Those Who Have Suffered a Miscarriage, Stillbirth, or Tubal Pregnancy (Pam Vredevelt)

Free to Grieve: Healing and Encouragement for Those Who Have Suffered Miscarriage and Stillbirth (Maureen Rank)

Grieving the Child I Never Knew (Kathe Wunnenberg)

I'll Hold You in Heaven (Jack Hayford)

Silent Grief: Miscarriage-Finding Your Way Through the Darkness (Clara Hinton)

When Your Baby Dies Through Miscarriage or Stillbirth (Ann T. Cooney and Louis A. Gamino)

Missions

Is That Really You, God? Hearing the Voice of God (Loren Cunningham)

Lifeguide Bible Studies: Missions (Cindi Bunch)

Operations World (Patrick Johnstone)

Short Term Mission's Workbook (Tim Dearborn)

Stepping Out: A Guide to Short Term Missions (YWAM)

Missions, Teen
Mission Trip Prep Kit Leader's Guide: Complete Preparation for Your Students' Cross-Cultural Experience (Kevin Johnson)

Mission Trip Prep: A Student Journal for Capturing the Experience (Kevin Johnson)

Names of God
Everything in the Bible: Every Name of God in the Bible (Larry Richards)

Intimate Moments with the Hebrew Names of God (Shmuel Wolkenfeld)

Lord, I Want to Know You: A Devotional Study on the Names of God (Kay Arthur)

Names of God Booklet

Names of God (Nathan Stone)

The Names of God (Kenneth Hemphill)

Names of God, Jesus
Names of Christ (James Bell)

Names of Jesus Leader's Guide (Elmer Towns)

New Believers
Basics for Believers (William Thrasher)

Beginning Your Christian Life (World Wide Publications)

Design for Discipleship: Your Life in Christ (Navigators)

First Steps for the New Christian (Christian Life Application Series) (AMG Publishers)

Growing in Christ (Navigators)

How to Begin the Christian Life (George Sweeting)

New Believers: Guide to Effective Christian Living (Greg Laurie)

New Christian's Handbook: Everything New Believers Need To Know (Max Anders)

So I'm a Christian, Now What? (Michael Simpson)

Starting Point Bible (Zondervan)

Studies in Christian Living Series: Knowing Jesus Christ (Navigators)

Your New Life in Christ (Luis Palau)

Parenting

7 Solutions for Burned-Out Parents (Dr. James Dobson)

A Chicken's Guide to Talking Turkey With Your Kids (Kevin Leman)

Boundaries with Kids (Henry Cloud and John Townsend)

Boundaries with Kids Workbook (Henry Cloud and John Townsend)

Helping Your Kids Deal With Anger, Fear and Sadness (Norm Wright)

How to Talk So Your Kids Will Listen (Norm Wright)

Prodigals and Those Who Love Them (Ruth Graham Bell)

Raising Pure Kids in an Impure World (Richard and Renee Durfield)

Parenting, Blended Families

The Stepfamily Survival Guide (Natalie Nichols Gillespie)

Parenting, Empty Nest

Give Them Wings (Carol Kuykendall)

The Second Half of Marriage: Facing the Eight Challenges of the Empty-Nest Years (David and Claudia Arp)

When You're Facing The Empty Nest: Avoiding Midlife Meltdown When Your Child Leaves Home (Mary Froehlich)

Parenting, Fathering

10 Things I Want My Son to Know: Getting Him Ready for Life (Steve Chapman)

Anchor Man (Steve Farrar)

Daughter Gone Wild, Dad's Gone Crazy (Charles and Heather Stone)

Fathering Like the Father (Kenneth Gangel and Howard Hendricks)

Raising a Modern Day Knight (Robert Lewis)

Survival Guide for New Dads: Two-Minute Devotions for Successful Fatherhood (Nick Harrison)

The Father Connection: 10 Qualities of the Heart That Empower Your Children to Make Right Choices (Josh McDowell)

To Own a Dragon: Reflections on Growing Up Without a Father (Donald Miller)

What A Daughter Needs from Her Dad (Michael Farris)

What a Difference a Daddy Makes (Kevin Leman)

Parenting, Grand-parenting

101 Ways to Love Your Grandkids (Bob and Emilie Barnes)

Off My Rocker: Grandparenting Ain't What It Used to Be (Gracie Malone)

The Gift of Grandparenting (Thea Jarvis)

The Gift of Grandparenting: Building Meaningful Relationships With Your Grandchildren (Eric Wiggin and Gary D. Chapman)

The Grandparents' Treasure Chest: A Journal of Memories to Share with Your Grandchildren (Edward Fays)

The Power of a Godly Grandparent: Building a Spiritual Inheritance for Your Grandchildren (Stephen Bly)

Parenting, Mothering

Daily Wisdom for Mothers (Michelle Adams)

Honey, Hang in There! Encouragement for Busy Moms (Sandra Picklesimer Aldrich)

Life Interrupted: The Scoop on Being a Young Mom (Tricia Goyer)

Lost Boys and the Moms Who Love Them: Encouragement and Hope for Dealing With Your Wayward Son (Melody Carlson)

Mom, I Feel Fat: Becoming Your Daughter's Ally in Developing a Healthy Body Image (Sharon Hersh)

Mom's Everything Book for Daughters (Becky Freeman)

Mom's Everything Book for Sons (Becky Freeman)

Mothers & Sons: Raising Boys to Be Men (Jean Lush)

Real Moms (Elisa Morgan)

Secrets of a Mid-Life Mom (Jane Jarrell)

The Greatest Mom Ever (Terri Camp)

The Heart of a Mother: True Stories of Inspiration and Encouragement (Mike Monte)

The Mom You're Meant to Be (Cheri Fuller)

The Power of a Positive Mom (Karol Ladd)

Parenting, New Baby

Before You Were Born (Nancy White Carlstrom)

I'm the Big Brother (Susan Ligon)

I'm the Big Sister (Susan Ligon)

My Baby Sister Is a Preemie (Helping Kids Heal) (Daina Amadeo)

Who's New at the Zoo? (Janette Oke)

Why Did You Bring Home a New Baby (Maribeth Boelts)

Parenting, New Moms

365 Things Every New Mom Should Know: A Daily Guide to Loving and Nurturing Your Child (Linda Danis)

First Time Mom (Kevin Leman)

Hugs for New Moms: Stories, Sayings and Scriptures to Encourage and Inspire the Heart (Stephanie Lynne)

O for a Thousand Nights to Sleep: An Eye-Opening Guide to the Wonder-Filled Months of Baby's First Year (Lorilee Craker)

Prayers for New and Expecting Moms (Michelle Howe)

Prayers for the Mother-to-Be (Angela Thomas)

Praying the Bible for Your Baby (Heather Harpham-Kopp)

Promises for Moms: From the New International Version (Zondervan)

Parenting, Pre-Teens

Preparing for Adolescence (Dr. James Dobson)

Preparing Your Daughter for Every Woman's Battle (Shannon Ethridge)

Preparing Your Son for Every Man's Battle (Stephen Arterburn)

So You Want to Be a Teenager? What Every Pre-Teen Must Know about Friends, Love, Sex, Dating and Other Life Issues (Dennis and Barbara Rainey)

Parenting, Single Parenting

A Comprehensive Guide to Parenting on Your Own (Lynda Hunter)

From One Single Mother to Another (Sandra Aldrich)

Successful Single Parenting (Gary Richmond)

The Single Dad's Survival Guide, How to Succeed as a One-Man Parenting Team (Mike Klumpp)

Tony Evans Speaks Out on Single Parenting (Tony Evans)

Parenting, Teens

Disarming the Teenage Heart (Jeff Leeland)

Helping Your Struggling Adolescent (Les Parrot)

How to Get Your Teen to Talk to You (Connie Grigsby)

How to Parent Your Teen Without Losing Your Mind (John McPherson)

Hurt: Inside the World of Today's Teenagers (Youth Edition) (Chap Clark)

I'm Pregnant... Now What? (Ruth Graham)

Mom and Dad I'm Pregnant: When Your Daughter or Son Faces an Unplanned Pregnancy (Jayne E. Schooler)

Mom, Eveyone Else Does! Becoming Your Daughters' Ally in Responding to Peer Pressure to Drink, Smoke and Use Drugs (Sharon Hersh)

Parenting the Wild Child (Miles McPherson)

Parenting Today's Adolescent (Dennis and Barbara Rainey)

Praying Prodigals Home (Quinn Sherrer)

Teenage Boys! Surviving and Enjoying These Extraordinary Years (William Beausay)

The Seven Cries of Today's Teen: Hearing Their Heart, Making a Connection (Tim Smith)

Why Christian Kids Rebel (Dr. Tim Kimmel)

Pre-Marital/Engagement

10 Great Dates Before You Say "I Do" (David and Claudia Arp)

101 Questions to Ask Before You Get Engaged (Norm Wright)

Pre-Marital/Engagement, Counseling

Before You Say "I Do:" A Marriage Preparation Manual for Couples (Norm Wright)

Getting Ready for Marriage (Jerry Hardin)

How Can I Be Sure: Questions to Ask Before You Get Married (Bob Phillips)

Preparing for Marriage God's Way (Wayne Mack)

Saving Your Marriage Before it Starts (Les Parrot)

Pre-Marital/Engagement, Devotional

Before You Say "I Do" Devotional (Norm Wright)

Devotions for Dating Couples: Building a Foundation for Spiritual intimacy (Ben Young)

Starting Out Together: A Devotional for Dating or Engaged Couples (Norm Wright)

Rape

Date Rape (Revised) (Ruth Goring)

Forgiving the Dead Man Walking (Debbie Morris)

Little Girl Lost (Nicky Cruz and Leisha Joseph)

Startling Beauty: A True Story of Rape and Grace (Heather Gemmen)

When Violence is No Stranger: Pastoral Counseling with Survivors of Acquaintance Rape (Kristen Leslie)

Relationships

Attachments: Why You Love, Feel and Act the Way You Do (Timothy Clinton)

Connecting (Dr. Larry Crabb)

Everybody's Normal Till You Get to Know Them (John Ortberg)

Love the Life You Live: 3 Secrets to Feeling Good (Les Parrot)

Pursuing Spiritual Transformation: Groups: The Life-Giving Power of Community (John Ortberg)

Relationships That Work (and Those That Don't) (Norm Wright)

Relationships: An Open and Honest Guide to Making Bad Relationships Better and Good Relationships Great (Les Parrot)

Safe People: How to Find Relationships That Are Good for You and Avoid Those That Aren't (Henry Cloud and John Townsend)

Sermon on the Mount: Connect with Others (Bill Hybels)

Unbreakable Bonds: Practicing the Art of Loving and Being Loved (Cheryl Meier and Paul Meier)

When You Love Too Much...Walking the Road to Health (Stephen Arterburn)

Who's Pushing Your Buttons? (Dr. John Townsend)

Relationships, Forgiveness

Finding Freedom in Forgiveness (Charles T. Jones)

Forgive and Forget: Healing the Hurts We Don't Deserve (Lewis Smedes)

Forgiveness: Making Peace with Your Past (Douglas Connelly)

Forgiving and Reconciling (Everett L. Worthington, Jr.)

Forgiving Our Parents, Forgiving Ourselves (Dr. David Stoop)

Forgiving the Unforgivable (David Stoop)

Show Each Other Forgiveness (Melody Carlson)

The Art of Forgiving: When You Need to Forgive and Don't Know How (Lewis Smedes)

The Choosing to Forgive Workbook (Les Carter and Frank Minirth)

The Gift of Forgiveness (Charles Stanley)

Total Forgiveness (R.T. Kendall)

When You Can't Say "I Forgive You:" Breaking the Bonds of Anger and Hurt (Grace Ketterman)

Relationships, Friendship

Authentic Relationships (Wayne and Clay Jacobsen)

Divine Secrets of Mentoring: Spiritual Growth Through Friendship (Carol Brazo)

Silver and Gold: Stories of Special Friendships (Linda Evans Shepherd)

The "Official" Friends Book (Martha Bolton)

The Friendship Factor: Revised, 25th Anniversary Edition (Alan McGinnis)

The Friendships of Women (Dee Brestin)

The Joy of Women's Friendships (Dee Brestin)

Treasured Friend: Finding and Keeping True Friendships (Ann Hibbard)

Relationships, Men
Men's Relational Toolbox (Gary Smalley)

Social Issues
How Can a Christian Be in Politics? (Roy Henron)

Naming the Unspeakable: Facing Up to Evil in an Age of Genocide and Terrorism (Os Guiness)

Social Issues, Aids
The AWAKE Project: Uniting against the African AIDS Crisis (Various Authors)

Social Issues, Cloning
Human Dignity in the Biotech Century: A Christian Vision for Public Policy (Charles Colson)

Life, Liberty and the Defense of Dignity: The Challenge for Bioethics (Leon Kaas)

Swindoll Leadership Library: Moral Dilemmas: Biblical Perspectives on Contemporary Ethical Issues (Charles Swindoll)

What Does the Bible Say about Cloning? (Dan Taylor)

Social Issues, Euthanasia
Christian Ethics: Options and Issues (Norman Geisler)

Issues of Conscience: Diaries on the Science & Sale of Life (Laurel Hughes)

Social Issues, Homosexuality
101 Frequently Asked Questions About Homosexuality (Mike Haley)

A Parent's Guide to Preventing Homosexuality (Dr. Joseph Nicolosi)

A Way of Escape: Freedom from Sexual Strongholds (Neil Anderson)

Coming Out of Homosexuality (Bob Davies)

Craving for Love: Relationship Addictions, Homosexuality and the God Who Heals (Brian Whitehead)

Dark Obsession: The Tragedy and Threat of the Homosexual Lifestyle (Timothy Dailey)

Desires in Conflict Updated (Joe Dallas)

Into the Promised Land: Beyond the Lesbian Struggle (Jeanette Howard)

Marriage On Trial: The Case Against Same Sex Marriage (Glenn Stanton)

Marriage Under Fire (James Dobson)

Our Social and Sexual Revolution: Major Issues for a New Century (John R.W. Stott)

Out of Egypt (Jeanette Howard)

Portraits of Freedom: 14 People Who Came Out of Homosexuality (Bob Davies)

Restoring Sexual Identity Hope for Women Who Struggle With Same-Sex Attraction (Anne Paulk)

Same Sex Partnership? A Christian Perspective (John R.W. Stott)

Someone I Love is Gay (Bob Davies)

The Facts on Homosexuality (John Ankerberg)

The Gay Agenda (Ronnie Floyd)

The Homosexual Agenda: Exposing the Principal Threat to Religious Freedom Today (Alan Sears)

The Same Sex Controversy: Defending and Clarifying the Bible's Message About Homosexuality (James White)

The Truth About Same Sex Marriage (Erwin Lutzer)

What's Wrong With Same-Sex Marriage? (James D. Kennedy)

When Homosexuality Hits Home (Joe Dallas)

Where Does a Mother Go to Resign? (Barbara Johnson)

Social Issues, Pacifism/War

When God Says War Is Right: The Christian's Perspective on When and How to Fight (Darrel Cole)

Why Does God Allow War? (David Martin Lloyd-Jones)

Why We Fight: Moral Clarity and the War on Terrorism (William J. Bennett)

Social Issues, Terrorism

Islam and Terrorism (Mark Gabriel)

Terrorism, Jihad and the Bible (John MacArthur)

When Worlds Collide: Where is God in Terrorism, War and Suffering? (R.C. Sproul)

Social Issues, Violence/Children

Angry Kids: Understanding and Managing the Emotions That Control Them (Richard Berry)

Kids Killing Kids (Linda Mintle)

Kids Who Kill: Confronting Our Culture of Violence (Mike Huckabee)

Social Issues, Violence/Teen

Chain Reaction: A Call to Compassionate Revolution (Steve Rabey)

Rachel Smiles: The Spiritual Legacy of Columbine Martyr Rachel Scott (Darrell Scott)

She Said Yes: The Unlikely Martyrdom of Cassie Bernall (Misty Bernall)

Suffering

A Bend in the Road: Experiencing God When Your World Caves In (David Jeremiah)

A Path Through Suffering: Discovering the Relationship Between God's Mercy and Our Pain (Elisabeth Elliott)

Am I Not Still God? (Kathy Troccoli)

Holding on to Hope (Nancy Guthrie)

Hope for the Troubled Heart (Billy Graham)

How Can It Be All Right When Everything is All Wrong? (Lewis Smedes)

How to Handle Adversity (Charles Stanley)

Real Survivors: Real-Life Stories of Hope for Difficult Times (Steve Bell)

Recovering from the Losses of Life (H. Norman Wright)

Suffering: Receiving God's Comfort (Jack Kuhatscheck)

The Gift of Pain (Paul Brand and Phillip Yancey)

The God of All Comfort: Devotions of Comfort, Strength & Hope for Those Who Chronically Suffer (Judy Gann)

The Problem of Pain (C.S. Lewis)

The Sword of Suffering: Enduring Words of Hope, Inspiration and Healing in the Midst of Despair (Stephen Olford)

When God Doesn't Heal Now (Larry Keefauver)

When God Doesn't Make Sense (Dr.James C. Dobson)

When God Weeps (Joni Earekson Tada)

When I Lay My Isaac Down (Carol Kent)

Where is God When It Hurts (Phillip Yancey)

Why Does God Allow Suffering? (Ralph Muncaster)

Wildflower Living: Cultivating Inner Strength During Times of Storm or Drought (Liz Morton Duckworth)

Suffering, Children

When Pete's Dad Got Sick: Helping Kids Heal (Kathleen Long Bostrom)

Suicide

Aftershock: Help, Hope and Healing in the Wake of Suicide (Arrington Cox)

An Eclipse of the Soul: A Christian Resource on Dealing with Suicide (Helen Koorman Hosier)

Bio Basics Series: Basic Questions on Suicide and Euthanasia: Are They Ever Right (Gary P. Stewart)

Finding Your Way After The Suicide of Someone You Love (David Biebel)

Grieving a Suicide: A Loved One's Search for Comfort, Answers & Hope (Albert Hsu)

Standing in the Shadow: Help and Encouragement for Suicide Survivors (June Cerza Kolf)

Suicide: A Christian Response: Crucial Considerations for Choosing Life (Timothy Demy)

Suicide, Teen

Friendship 911: Thoughts of Suicide (Josh McDowell)

Parent's Guide to Top 10 Dangers Teens Face (Stephen Arterburn)

Real Teens, Real Stories, Real Life (Suzanne Eller)

Women's Issues

Captivating (John and Stasi Eldredge)

Every Woman's Battle (Stephen Arterburn)

Every Young Woman's Battle (Shannon Ethridge)

The Allure of Hope (Jan Meyers)